www.wadsworth.com

www.wadsworth.com is the World Wide Web site
for Wadsworth and is your direct source to dozens
of online resources.

At *www.wadsworth.com* you can find out about
supplements, demonstration software, and student
resources. You can also send email to many of our
authors and preview new publications and exciting
new technologies.

www.wadsworth.com

Changing the way the world learns®

From the Wadsworth Series in Mass Communication and Journalism

General Mass Communication

Anokwa/Lin/Salwen, *International Communication: Issues and Controversies*

Biagi, *Media/Impact: An Introduction to Mass Media*, Sixth Edition

Bucy, *Living in the Information Age: A New Media Reader*

Craft/Leigh/Godfrey, *Electronic Media*

Day, *Ethics in Media Communications: Cases and Controversies*, Fourth Edition

Dennis/Merrill, *Media Debates: Great Issues for the Digital Age*, Third Edition

Gillmor/Barron/Simon, *Mass Communication Law: Cases and Comment*, Sixth Edition

Gillmor/Barron/Simon/Terry, *Fundamentals of Mass Communication Law*

Hilmes, *Connections: A Broadcast History Reader*

Hilmes, *Only Connect: A Cultural History of Broadcasting in the United States*

Jamieson/Kohrs Campbell, *The Interplay of Influence: News, Advertising, Politics, and the Mass Media*, Fifth Edition

Kamalipour, *Global Communication*

Lester, *Visual Communication: Images with Messages*, Third Edition

Overbeck, *Major Principles of Media Law*, 2004 Edition

Sparks, *Media Effects Research: A Basic Overview*

Straubhaar/LaRose, *Media Now: Understanding Media, Culture, and Technology*, Fourth Edition

Zelezny, *Communications Law: Liberties, Restraints, and the Modern Media*, Fourth Edition

Zelezny, *Cases in Communications Law*, Fourth Edition

Journalism

Bowles/Borden, *Creative Editing*, Fourth Edition

Chance/McKeen, *Literary Journalism: A Reader*

Fischer, *Sports Journalism at Its Best: Pulitzer Prize-Winning Articles, Cartoons, and Photographs*

Fisher, *The Craft of Corporate Journalism*

Gaines, *Investigative Reporting for Print and Broadcast*, Second Edition

Hilliard, *Writing for Television, Radio, and New Media*, Eighth Edition

Kessler/McDonald, *When Words Collide: A Media Writer's Guide to Grammar and Style*, Sixth Edition

Klement/Matalene, *Telling Stories/Taking Risks: Journalism Writing at the Century's Edge*

Laakaniemi, *Newswriting in Transition*

Miller, *Power Journalism: Computer-Assisted Reporting*

Rich, *Writing and Reporting News: A Coaching Method*, Fourth Edition

Rich, *Writing and Reporting News: A Coaching Method, Student Exercise Workbook*, Fourth Edition

Wilber/Miller, *Modern Media Writing*

Photojournalism and Photography

Parrish, *Photojournalism: An Introduction*

Public Relations and Advertising

Diggs-Brown/Glou, *The PR Styleguide: Formats for Public Relations Practice*

Hendrix, *Public Relations Cases*, Sixth Edition

Jewler/Drewniany, *Creative Strategy in Advertising*, Seventh Edition

Newsom/Carrell, *Public Relations Writing: Form and Style*, Sixth Edition

Newsom/Turk/Kruckeberg, *This Is PR: The Realities of Public Relations*, Eighth Edition

Sivulka, *Soap, Sex, and Cigarettes: A Cultural History of American Advertising*

Woods, *Advertising and Marketing to the New Majority: A Case Study Approach*

Research and Theory

Baxter/Babbie, *The Basics of Communication Research*

Baran/Davis, *Mass Communication Theory: Foundations, Ferment, and Future*, Third Edition

Littlejohn, *Theories of Human Communication*, Seventh Edition

Rubenstein, *Surveying Public Opinion*

Wimmer/Dominick, *Mass Media Research: An Introduction*, Seventh Edition

When Words Collide

A Media Writer's Guide to Grammar and Style

Sixth Edition

Lauren Kessler
University of Oregon

Duncan McDonald
University of Oregon

THOMSON
™
WADSWORTH

Australia • Canada • Mexico • Singapore • Spain
United Kingdom • United States

THOMSON

WADSWORTH

Publisher: Holly J. Allen
Assistant Editor: Nicole George
Editorial Assistant: Shona Burke
Technology Project Manager:
Jeanette Wiseman
Marketing Manager: Kimberly Russell
Marketing Assistant: Neena Chandra
Advertising Project Manager: Shemika Britt
Project Manager, Editorial Production:
Mary Noel

Print/Media Buyer: Doreen Suruki
Permissions Editor: Sarah Harkrader
Production Service: Melanie Field,
Strawberry Field Publishing
Text Designer: Wendy LaChance
Copy Editor: Elizabeth von Radics
Cover Designer: Preston Thomas
Compositor: TBH Typecast, Inc.
Text and Cover Printer: Transcontinental
Printing, Inc., Louiseville, QC

For more information about our products, contact us at:
Thomson Learning Academic Resource Center
1-800-423-0563
For permission to use material from this text, contact us by
Phone: 1-800-730-2214
Fax: 1-800-730-2215
Web: http://www.thomsonrights.com

Library of Congress Control Number:
2002117699

Student Edition with InfoTrac College Edition:
ISBN 0-534-56206-X

Student Edition without InfoTrac College Edition:
ISBN 0-534-56211-6

Wadsworth Group/
Thomson Learning
10 Davis Drive
Belmont, CA 94002-3098
USA

Asia
Thomson Learning
5 Shenton Way #01-01
UIC Building
Singapore 068808

Australia/New Zealand
Thomson Learning
102 Dodds Street
South Melbourne, Victoria 3006
Australia

Canada
Nelson
1120 Birchmount Road
Toronto, Ontario M1K 5G4
Canada

Europe/Middle East/Africa
Thomson Learning
High Holborn House
50/51 Bedford Row
London WC1R 4LR
United Kingdom

Latin America
Thomson Learning
Seneca, 53
Colonia Polanco
11560 Mexico D.F.
Mexico

Spain/Portugal
Paraninfo
Calle/Magallanes, 25
28015 Madrid, Spain

CONTENTS

PREFACE

What we communicate—and *how* we do it—reflects on us personally and professionally.

For those dedicated and fortunate (and maybe foolhardy) enough to become professional writers, the challenge is profound: to employ language carefully, purposefully and gracefully; to find words—the right words—and use them to spark ideas and ignite emotions, to capture experience and tell stories. Underneath this art of communication lies a clear knowledge of the way language works, the patterns and rules and shared conventions that allow us to transmit ideas across time and space. Underneath lies grammar.

The job we've set out to accomplish in "When Words Collide" is to put you on intimate terms with grammar so you can write well. It's that simple. There are those who find the study of grammar endlessly fascinating. We're not in that crowd. We're writers who understand that the better we know the tools of our trade—words and how to use them—the better writers we will be. We don't *love* grammar. We *need* it. We can get frustrated, just like you do, with its intricacies and inconsistencies, its sometimes-finicky rules and occasionally exasperating exceptions. But we know that the reward for mastering grammar is being able to write with clarity, power and grace—and that's quite a reward.

It is in this spirit that we offer the sixth edition of "When Words Collide." We want you to learn grammar not for its own sake but because it is central to good writing and effective communication. As our own careers as writers and teachers have progressed through the years, our commitment to this idea has only deepened.

Your decision to read this book shows that you share that commitment. Congratulations. You've already taken the first big step toward improving your writing. Let us—let "When Words Collide"—help you along the way.

We think this edition of "When Words Collide" is even stronger and more useful than its predecessors. We've expanded and clarified, edited and polished. We've added new chapters, new examples and new entries. Here are some specifics:

- A new "quick-start" Chapter 1: "Ten Secrets to Writing Well"

- The former first chapter—now Chapter 2—provides a strong focus on connecting clear writing to good grammar

- A new, separate chapter on the verb and appropriate uses, giving this important subject matter ample coverage

- A spelling chapter refocused on language and literacy, seeing versus hearing and the dangers of software spell-checkers

- New coverage on ethnic stereotyping in Chapter 13 (formerly chapter 11)

- Numerous new examples to keep the text current and engaging.

- A new Web site with exercises and activities to enhance the text and exercises workbook by providing numerous tutorial opportunities: http://communication.wadsworth.com/kessler

We continue to bring the challenges of our own writing lives to these pages, hoping this book will find a permanent place by your side as you learn and perfect the art of communication.

ACKNOWLEDGMENTS

We thank the following reviewers for their ideas and comments: Tom Clanin, California State University, Fullerton; Steve J. Collins, University of Texas, Arlington; Betsy Leebron, Temple University; and Tim Pilgrim, Western Washington University. We also thank the many teachers around the country who have class-tested and enthusiastically supported "When Words Collide" during its almost 20-year tenure. And we thank the thousands of students who have struggled with the complexities of the English language on the road to becoming professional writers. It is to them, and to our families, that we dedicate this book.

Lauren Kessler
Duncan McDonald
Eugene, Oregon

When
Words
Collide

A Media Writer's Guide
to Grammar and Style

PART 1

Understanding Grammar and Style

CHAPTER 1

Ten Secrets
to Writing Well

We call this book a "guide to grammar and style," but it is really a guide to writing well. That's because grammar—the set of rules that govern the use of language—is the cornerstone of good writing.

Don't think of grammar as a litany of rules meant to confuse or constrain you—or, worse yet, to be learned in isolation, outside the act of writing. Think of grammar as the instruction manual that will help you master the tools of the writer's trade: words, phrases, sentences, paragraphs. We're not saying that knowing grammar will automatically transform you into a great writer any more than knowing the rules and rudiments of basketball will transform you into Shaquille O'Neal. We are saying, simply, that the rules underlay the game—and the game is writing well. So, before we start with the rules, let's remember *why* we are learning them in the first place. Let's remember the game. Let's focus for a moment on what it takes to write well.

Are there really *10* secrets to writing well? Maybe there is only one— truly caring about writing and making it a priority in your life—but we think these others will help you along the path. Here are our 10 secrets.

1. READ

Reading is not just a way to find out about the world, or yourself; it is an immersion in language. Whether you read a biology textbook or a sci-fi thriller, a news magazine or a detective novel, you are swimming in words, awash in sentences, carried along by a stream of paragraphs. Whether you know it or not, you are learning language along with whatever else you are reading. You are learning vocabulary and syntax, words and how they are put together. You are learning how language flows (or doesn't).

The lessons can be positive and obvious, as when you marvel at a passage that transports you to another time or place or when, in midparagraph, you feel in the grip of ideas or emotions. That's a writer forging a connection with words, and it's a lesson you take with you, consciously or not, after you close the book or put away the magazine. The more you read, the more you have these experiences, the more embedded becomes the beauty and the precision of language. Of course, the lessons can be negative as well—the book that puts you to sleep midpage, the newspaper story you stop reading after the first paragraph. You are learning something here too: You are learning what doesn't work, how not to put words together, how not to tell a story.

Imagine wanting to be a musician and not listening to music. That's as odd and wrongheaded as aspiring to be a writer and not reading.

2. HAVE SOMETHING TO SAY

That sounds too obvious, doesn't it? But how many times have you sat in front of your computer screen, vision blurred, mind numb, unable to write a single intelligent sentence? You tell yourself you have writer's block. You don't have writer's block. You are more likely suffering from a dearth of material, a paucity of ideas—the lack of something to say. Perhaps you haven't worked your ideas through in your head. You aren't clear about what you think. Or maybe you haven't done the necessary research. You don't know your subject well enough yet. You can't write well if you are not in command of the material. You can't write well if you don't know what you want to say.

Consider how all of us, at times, are reduced to babbling. We open our mouths, but our lips are working faster than our brains. Words come out. We sputter, stop and start, ramble, backtrack, circumlocute. The lips keep moving, but there is little sense and less meaning behind the words because we haven't stopped to figure out what we want to say. Friends may indulge us, but readers don't. Readers just stop reading.

3. ORGANIZE YOUR THOUGHTS

Without an organizational plan, writing well is much more difficult than it needs to be. It is not, however, impossible. You can write without a plan if you want to rewrite and revise and restructure many times over. But it is much more sensible, more efficient and decidedly less stressful to think about how you will structure the piece—be it advertising copy or a magazine article—before you begin writing. Some media forms have their own internal structure and provide a kind of template you can use. Basic news stories are like that. So are press releases. Advertising copy also often follows a certain pattern. But even if the template is provided, you need to organize your thoughts and your material within it. And so, determined to write well, you sit with the material, review everything, underline important elements, jot notes to yourself in the margins, look up missing details, perhaps make a few phone calls. You don't rush to write. You take the time to understand the material. From that understanding can come all kinds of good ideas about how to structure the piece.

How should you organize? For short pieces, you may be able to keep everything in your head. But most writers who know what they're doing don't trust this method. They depend on notes. Some do fine with key words and phrases scribbled on scraps of paper. Others prefer writing full outlines. Some use the computer to organize, putting their notes into a database that's accessible, and sortable, in countless ways. Others like to use file cards, one idea to a card, which can be shuffled and reshuffled as the writer thinks through the piece.

4. CONSIDER YOUR AUDIENCE

Unlike your journal or your diary or the letters or emails you send to friends and family, media messages are meant for public consumption. But what public? How can you write well if you don't know who will be reading or listening? You can't—or at the very least you stack the deck against it. It's not just that media messages are more effective when they are targeted, when the writer knows who the audience is. It's also a matter of the writing itself—the words you use, the approach you take. If you don't know the audience, you are not sure what your readers or viewers or listeners know or need to know. You are not sure how to approach these folks, what level of vocabulary to employ, what tone to choose, how to structure what you want to say. Should you use humor? Will irony work? Who knows—if you don't know your audience.

That's why companies fund market research: to see who is out there and how best to reach them. That's why magazines conduct readership studies or run surveys to gauge what their readers think about certain issues. Knowing the audience is a key to good writing.

5. KNOW GRAMMATICAL CONVENTIONS AND KNOW HOW TO USE THEM

Here we are, back to the rules of the game. Note that knowing the rules becomes important only when you have something to say, figure out how you're going to say it and know to whom you're talking. The rules themselves—memorizing verb forms or knowing when to use a comma—don't exist without a context. The context is writing. You learn the rules for one reason: to play the game.

Writing well means making countless good decisions, from choosing just the right word (see #6) to crafting phrases and clauses and sentences and paragraphs that say just what you want them to say, with precision, clarity and grace (see #7). This lofty but achievable goal is possible only if you understand the architecture of language, the building blocks of prose, if you are at ease with the tools of the trade. Imagine a potter who has a wonderful idea for a vase but has not mastered the wheel. Imagine a carpenter who can't use a skill saw, a dancer who doesn't know the steps, a Web site designer who can't write HTML. That's a writer without a command of grammar. We have more to say on this in Chapter 2.

6. MASTER A SOLID WORKING VOCABULARY

Sculptors have clay; painters have paint; writers have words. It's as simple as that. Writers have to figure out how to connect with an audience—how to inform, educate, entertain, tell a story, set a scene, promote a product, sell an idea—and all they have are words. But words are one of the most potent tools around, perhaps *the* most potent. What variety, what nuance, what tone! Words carry not only meaning but shades of meaning. Look up *talk* in a thesaurus and you will find *chatter, mutter, mumble, gossip* and *schmooze,* each with its own connotation, each with its own feel. And words not only have meaning and nuance but also sound and rhythm.

Building a good vocabulary means reading widely. It means both appreciating the smorgasbord that is the English language and learning to use words with proper respect—that is, choosing the correct word, the word that means exactly what *you* mean, and spelling it correctly. Building a vocabulary does not mean seeking out multisyllabic tongue twisters or collecting fancy or elaborate expressions. It means being able to use words like *chatter, mutter, mumble, gossip* and *schmooze* when called for.

7. FOCUS ON PRECISION AND CLARITY

If you think clear, crisp writing just flows naturally from the fingertips of the writer to the computer screen, you couldn't be more wrong. Writing with precision and clarity—saying exactly what you mean, no more, no less, no fuzziness, no confusion, no second or third reading—is hard, purposeful work. But it's work your readers, viewers or listeners expect you to do. If you don't, they turn the page or reach for the remote, and whatever you had to say, whatever you thought you were communicating, is lost.

Clear, powerful writing is the result of good decisions, from choosing the right word to crafting just the right construction to relentlessly slashing clutter from your prose. Redundancies? Euphemisms? Jargon? These are obstacles to precision. Misplaced modifiers? Split constructions? Run-on sentences? These are the enemies of clarity. In fact, every grammatical decision you make either enhances or detracts from clarity. That's how important a working knowledge of grammar is to writing well. That's how careful you must learn to be if you want to write clearly and crisply.

8. HEAR LANGUAGE

"Write for the ear," broadcasters are often told, but this is good advice for *all* writers. It doesn't matter whether the audience actually hears aloud the words you write or just "hears" your prose when reading silently. In either case, the audience attends to the sound and feels the beat of the language. If you can master the skill of writing for the ear, you are one step closer to writing well.

Listen to the words you use. What meaning is conveyed by their sound? Listen to how words sound together. Do they fight one another? Do they flow? Say your written sentences out loud. Do they have a rhythm? A long sentence can be breathless and lilting with its own forward, rolling motion. A short, choppy sentence can set a quick pace or tap out a staccato beat. Purposeful repetition of words or phrases can add rhythm as can the emphatic use of parallel structure. Mastering the aural nuances and subtleties of language is one of the joys of writing.

9. REVISE

Think you're finished once you write it all down? Think all you have to do is a quick once-over, a spell-check and it's out the door? Think again. Having the patience and fortitude—and humility—to *really* revise is what separates the amateurs from the professionals. Revision is much more than tidying up, pruning and polishing prose. It is an opportunity to see if the writing works. It is a chance to rethink what you are trying to say. Consider the word *revision: re-vision—to look again, to look with new eyes.* This is what the revision process should be.

And so thoughtful writers, determined to produce clear, powerful, even memorable prose, take a deep breath after they have "finished" whatever it is they were writing. Now it is time to revise. It is time to look at the piece and ask: Does it say what I intended it to say? Will my readers or viewers or listeners learn what I want them to learn? Have I written enough or too much? Do the ideas flow from one to another? Do my transitions work? Does my style fit both the subject and the audience? Taking revision seriously means asking the tough questions and being prepared to spend the extra time to answer them.

Even with the best intentions, it is very difficult to learn the art of revision on your own work. You *know* what you mean even if you don't *write* what you mean. Thus, when you read your own work, you read what you know you meant and not necessarily what you have written. It may be that learning how to revise is best accomplished by revising others' writing. It is much easier to see the shortcomings of other people's work, the holes in their logic, the sputtering of their prose, the clutter, the murkiness. It is also true that you often see in others your own problems or shortcomings. With practice and over time, if you stay humble and audience-directed, you can learn to be more clear-eyed about your work.

10. APPLY THE SEAT OF THE PANTS TO THE SEAT OF THE CHAIR

The final secret to writing well is the easiest to state and the hardest to accomplish: Put in the time. Just like mastering a musical instrument or a new sport, learning to write takes practice—lots of practice; this means time—good, concentrated, focused time over weeks and months and, yes, even years. Some people seem to have a natural facility with words (probably because they are voracious readers). Others struggle more. But everyone who wants to write well, talent notwithstanding, has to work hard at it. It is easy to get discouraged. It is easy to get distracted. It is easy to talk away your enthusiasm over coffee with friends. Sometimes it feels as if it's easy to do just about anything *other* than write. You have to rein yourself in. Give yourself a pep talk. Get back to your desk. As the poet Marge Piercy has wisely written: A real writer is one who really writes.

 For online activities, go to the Web site for this book at *http://communication.wadsworth.com/kessler.*

CHAPTER 2

What You Don't Know
Will Hurt You

Grammar is not rocket science. True, the English language can be challenging. As writers—and readers—we wouldn't want it otherwise, would we? And yes, there is much to learn on the way to mastering the rules that govern how we write. But there is no reason to be intimidated. We human beings are prewired to do this kind of work. Communication is our claim to fame, evolutionarily speaking. We're good at this. But those of us who want to be writers have to be *very* good at this.

That's where grammar comes in. Grammar makes communication possible. Without the shared conventions of grammar, without the structure it creates and the patterns it plots, we could not speak to one another across time and space. Grammar is the writer's touchstone, our ritual. It binds us together whether we write journal entries or journalism, haiku or press releases, whether our book is number one on the New York Times best-seller list or we have just registered for our first writing class.

We know that grammar has a bad rap: It's confusing. It's picky. It's fussy. There are almost as many exceptions as there are rules. And it's, well, *unnecessary*, isn't it? "I never learned grammar in school, but it hasn't hurt me yet," you say. "I can always write around what I don't know," you insist. "Hey, it's the ideas that count, not the grammar," you declare.

Sorry. Wrong on all counts.

First of all, grammar is not all that confusing. In fact, it is mostly logical and orderly, often commonsensical and very accessible (that's right: not rocket science). Most of the rules are straightforward, and, happily, good grammar almost always *sounds right* to those who read and have the patterns of prose embedded in their brains. Second, grammar is absolutely necessary, not only to writing clearly but also to writing with style and creativity and pizzazz.

Consider this comment from journalist, essayist, novelist and screenwriter Joan Didion, one of the finest prose stylists writing today: "All I know about grammar is its infinite power," she writes. "To shift the structure of a sentence alters the meaning of that sentence, as definitely and inflexibly as the position of a camera alters the meaning of the object photographed. Many people know about cameras today, but not so many know about sentences."

But we *must* know about sentences, about phrases, clauses, voices, tenses, singulars, plurals—all the patterns and constructions that make our language work. Language is how we spread ideas and information throughout society. The information we have to communicate as writers may be complex; the ideas may be challenging. The message will have to compete with countless distractions for the attention of the audience. This puts a tremendous burden on the language: It must be crisp and clear, easy to understand and inviting. It must carry the ideas effortlessly, even gracefully. It must enhance meaning. It must communicate tone and nuance, color and texture, sound and rhythm. But to do all this, the language must be—before all else—correct. It must be grammatical.

All languages depend on rules of grammar, although these conventions may not be entirely evident to outsiders. Nonstandard English defies many of the rules of conventional English, but it has patterns of its own, linguistic conventions that guide its use. So too does sign language, where grammar occurs in the eyes, the brows, the tilt of the head, the lips. Just as sentence construction communicates meaning in written English, a tucked chin, narrowed eyes or raised shoulders act as grammatical signposts in the language of the deaf. Even baby talk has its own simple grammar ("Me want milk!").

Face it: Grammar is everywhere.

THE WRITER AS ARTISAN AND ARTIST

Consider writing a craft, like carpentry. Just as a builder of fine furniture wouldn't attempt to build a cabinet using a dull saw and rusty nails, neither would a writer try to create a memorable passage using clichés and clumsy constructions. Artisans care about—and for—the tools of their trade, just as writers must. Think of learning grammar as learning how to use these tools and learning to choose the right tool for the job.

If you would rather think of yourself as an artist than an artisan, consider that artists too pay particular attention to fundamentals, to the basic tools they will use to create their art. The painter studies color; the musician learns scales; the actor takes classes in voice control and body movement. These fundamentals are not the art itself, just as grammar is not writing, but they are the means to mastery. Whether you consider writing an art or a craft or a bit of both, it is clear that you need to start with and build from the basics.

Artists, of course, occasionally break the rules to purposefully, even gleefully, defy the conventions of their own medium. Writers do this, too. Think of William Faulkner's sentences of 100-plus words, grammatical run-ons that make you breathless and dizzy while they transport you to a world that exists only in the author's imagination. He did this consciously, with full knowledge of the rules. He knew the patterns and conventions of language so well that he could play with them. Clearly, some rules can be broken to create special effects, but they must be *known* before they can be flouted.

MAKING MISTAKES

What is exciting and challenging about learning to write well is that it is a lifelong process. Throughout our lives as writers, we will grow, we will change and, inevitably, we will make mistakes: judgments miscalled, questions unasked and language misused. Errors can be disheartening, not to mention embarrassing.

Grammatical errors are particularly dangerous to the professional lives of writers. "If I see a misspelled word on a résumé or a grammatical error, I look no further. I immediately disqualify the applicant," says the personnel director of a large company. "We look at how much attention a person pays to detail," says the vice president of a major advertising firm. "Things like grammar, spelling and mechanics mean a lot to us. We figure, if the person can't accomplish these things, how can we expect him or her to move on to bigger jobs?" Says a newspaper editor: "If I find grammatical and mechanical errors in the first paragraph, I stop reading. If a person can't use grammar correctly, it says either of two things to me—lack of intelligence or extreme sloppiness. Either way, it's not the person I want writing for me." A magazine editor agrees: "We get hundreds of email queries, writers proposing stories for us. For some reason, people think it's okay to write poorly when they write an email. We don't think so at all. We would never hire a writer freelance if that person emailed us a query with grammatical or spelling errors. And it's amazing how many of them do."

But mistakes do happen. It is precisely because professional writers know this—and understand the unpleasant consequences of making errors publicly—that they take *editing* so seriously. They begin with a solid understanding of the language and then they edit, edit, edit. The misspelled word, the misplaced modifier, the lack of parallelism, the shift in voice—all the little errors that can creep into writing never make it past the editing process. It is here experienced writers turn their uncertain, sometimes ragged prose into the polished material they can proudly present to their audience.

WHAT YOU DON'T KNOW . . .

What you don't know *will* hurt you. It will hurt the clarity of your writing, the understanding and respect of your audience, even your ability to land a job in the first place. What is it you don't know? Let's consider 10 of the most common grammatical mistakes and how knowledge of the language (and reading this book) can help you avoid them.

Mistake #1: Thinking you don't have to know grammar to write well.   After reading this far, you certainly won't make this mistake again, will you?

Mistake #2: Subjects and verbs that don't agree.   For a sentence to be grammatically correct and clearly communicative, a verb must agree with the intended number of its subject. That sounds simple, as in: *The book* [singular subject] *is* [singular verb] *in the library* or *The books* [plural subject] *are* [plural verb] *on the reading list.* But it gets complicated when you're not quite sure what the subject is. There may be a number of nouns and pronouns in the sentence. Which is the true subject? There may be confusion about the intended number of the verb. *Five thousand dollars,* as a subject, looks plural but acts singular; *everyone* clearly implies the plural but acts as a singular subject. To sort this all out, you need to know the parts of speech (Chapters 3 and 4), the parts of a sentence (Chapter 5) and the guidelines for agreement (Chapter 6).

Mistake #3: Subjects and pronouns that don't agree.   To communicate crisply and clearly, sentences must have internal harmony. Just as subjects and verbs must agree, so too must subjects and their pronouns. Adhering to this straightforward rule depends on your ability to identify the subject, recognize its number and choose a corresponding pronoun. This can be simple, as in: *The books* [plural subject] *and their* [plural pronoun] *authors.* Or it can be tougher, as in: *Everyone should remain in (their/his or her) seat* or *The team made (their/its) way to the locker room.* But if you understand the parts of speech (Chapters 3 and 4) and the guidelines for agreement (Chapter 6), you should be able to avoid this pitfall.

Mistake #4: Lack of parallelism.   To be both coherent and forceful, a sentence must have parallel structure; that is, its elements must be in balance. Consider a construction like *I came. I saw. I conquered.* It is powerful because it sets out three ideas in three parallel grammatical structures (pronoun–past-tense verb). Consider the same idea expressed this way: *I came. I looked over everything. The enemy was conquered by my armies.* That's lack of parallelism. That's bad writing. You have to know the parts of speech (Chapters 3 and 4) to understand the concept of parallelism and you must see parallelism as a form of agreement (Chapter 6).

Mistake #5: Confusing *who* and *whom*.   *Who/whom did the president name to his cabinet? She voted for whoever/whomever endorsed the treaty. The judge who/whom tried the case refused to speak with reporters.* Confused? You won't be once you understand the nominative and objective cases (Chapter 7).

Mistake #6: Confusing *that* and *which*.   Did you think these two words were interchangeable? Well, they aren't. Consider this sentence: *The readership poll that/which the magazine commissioned helped shape editorial policy. That* is used to introduce material that restricts the meaning of the noun; *which* is used to elaborate on meaning. If you know about relative pronouns (Chapter 4) and the role of phrases and clauses in a sentence (Chapter 5), you will use these words correctly.

Mistake #7: Confusing possessives and contractions.   That's a fancy way of saying that *your* (possessive) and *you're* (contraction) are not interchangeable. They perform very different tasks in a sentence. *Their* and *they're, whose* and *who's, its* and *it's* may sound the same, but they do not have the same grammatical functions. Learning parts of speech (Chapter 4) and case (Chapter 7) will end the confusion.

Mistake #8: Dangling and misplacing modifiers.   A misplaced modifier (a word, phrase or clause) does not point clearly and directly to what it is supposed to modify. A modifier "dangles" when what it is supposed to modify is not part of the sentence. Both grammatical errors seriously compromise clarity of meaning. If you understand parts of speech (Chapters 3 and 4) and parts of the sentence (Chapter 5), this clarity, conciseness and coherence issue (Chapter 11) will make sense.

Mistake #9: Misusing commas. Some novice writers just don't take commas seriously enough, sprinkling them throughout sentences like decoration, figuring "when in doubt, put one in." But commas have specific functions in a sentence, as do all marks of punctuation. In addition to generally overusing commas, writers frequently fall prey to two other comma errors. One is neglecting to use a comma to separate two independent clauses linked by a coordinating conjunction. The other, ironically, is using only a comma when trying to link two independent clauses (known as the *comma-splice error*). If some of this terminology is foreign to you, it won't be after you read about parts of speech (Chapter 4), the sentence (Chapter 5) and punctuation (Chapter 9).

Mistake #10: The dreaded passive voice. Do you know what the passive voice is? You will, after reading Chapter 8. It is one of the surest ways to suck the life out of a sentence and construct stilted, falsely formal or bureaucratic prose. Although passive voice construction is not technically a grammatical error and although there are a few defensible reasons for using it, most passive-voice sentences are not written knowingly or purposefully. Both the clarity (Chapter 11) and the liveliness (Chapter 12) of writing are at stake.

All these grammatical hazards—we could list hundreds more—may seem daunting. Don't be daunted. Be respectful. Understand that language is alive, complex, fascinating—and full of potential pitfalls. That doesn't mean you should be intimidated. It means you should be careful. It means you should learn the tools of your trade. It means you should study the fundamentals and build a writing life from this firm foundation. "When Words Collide" can help.

THE POINT OF GRAMMAR

The point of grammar is *not* grammar. The point is writing. Grammar is only the road map. The destination is clear, concise, compelling prose. Grammar is only the rule book. You learn the rules not so you can parrot the rules, not so you can be an expert on the rules, not so you can pass a test on the rules, but so you can play the game. The game is writing. Don't forget that. Don't ever lose sight of *why* you're learning grammar, why you're learning the rules—and why you're reading this book.

The study of grammar is more than the study of the rules and regulations that give order and structure to the language. The study of grammar is the key to the power of words. Read on. Write on.

 For online activities, go to the Web site for this book at *http://communication.wadsworth.com/kessler.*

CHAPTER 3

Parts of Speech, Part 1:
The Power of the Verb

The *word*. That's what *verb* means in Latin, and that very definition reveals its power and its function. The verb is at the core of all writing: It propels, it positions, it pronounces.

If you can picture a sentence as an inventory of parts on an automotive assembly line, imagine the verb as both the engine and the steering wheel for the soon-to-be-completed "vehicle." That sentence goes nowhere without the verb. It can't even start!

As the powertrain for all writing, the verb drives the machinery that organizes and directs all the words we use in our language. We call this organization *parts of speech*. Every word in a dictionary falls into one or more category, indicating its role and function in a sentence. We begin our discussion of the parts of speech with a focus on the verb. In Chapter 4 we discuss the noun, pronoun, adjective, adverb, preposition, conjunction and the somewhat eccentric interjection. As we observe in that chapter, an understanding of the parts of speech—and how they interact—is essential to your mastery of grammar.

So, on to the verb—let's inspect and dissect this powerful tool.

VERB FUNCTIONS

In most writing, a verb states an *action* or *effort:*

The auditors <u>criticized</u> the company's accounting methods.

The company president <u>resigned</u> this morning.

Verbs also indicate a *state of being:*

Stockholders <u>are</u> angry about the latest accounting revelations.

In all three examples, the verb drives or directs the sentence.

VERB FORMS

The three sentences under "Verb Functions" illustrate three forms of verbs: transitive, intransitive and linking. Understanding these forms is key to making correct choices as to case (Chapter 7), to preventing the use of an adverb where an adjective belongs and to avoiding errors with such troublesome verb pairs as *lay/lie* and *sit/set*. There are many more reasons to understand them, as you will soon discover.

1. **Transitive verb.** In Latin *trans* means "through" or "across." In grammar the transitive verb carries *action* from the subject to the object, as in:

   The <u>auditors</u> <u>criticized</u> the company's accounting <u>methods</u>.
       (subj.)   (verb)   (obj.)

(criticized <u>what?</u>)

This sentence clearly shows an action being transported from the initiator of the action (auditors) to its target (accounting methods) or, pardon the pun, to the object of the criticism. So, in transitive verb constructions, you will have the verb "answering" *what?* or *whom?* (criticized what? or criticized whom?). These recipients of action are called *direct objects*. Another example:

   <u>Auditors</u> <u>challenged</u> the <u>president</u> to explain the discrepancies.
   (subj.)   (trans. verb)   (dir. obj.)

(challenged <u>whom?</u>)

2. **Intransitive verb.** As the prefix *in* suggests, this verb form is *not* transitive. Although there is no recipient of any action from this type of verb, sentences with intransitive verbs do convey action as well as *location* or a *state of being*. Example:

   Company <u>shares</u> <u>fell</u> sharply this morning in heavy trading.
           (subj.) (intrans. verb)

Note that in intransitive verb constructions, the words following the verb don't answer the question *what?;* they reply to *how?* or *when?* Another example:

   The <u>company</u> <u>will file</u> for bankruptcy protection this morning.
       (subj.)   (intrans. verb)

You can see that although this verb form conveys action, it can indicate location or position as well, which sometimes causes this form to be confused with the linking verb (which we discuss next). In this example:

The <u>suspect</u> <u>was</u> in the alley when police surrounded him.
(subj.) (intrans. verb)

the verb, a form of *to be,* suggests only location, not a specific characterization of the subject (which the linking verb form would convey). This sentence illustrates that not all *to be* constructions are linking verbs.

3. **Linking verb.** This verb form may seem weak compared with its grammatical siblings, but it has an important role in *linking* the subject with a modifier, which enhances the meaning or description of that subject. Example:

The company's <u>stock</u> <u>is</u>   <u>worthless.</u>
(subj.)(l. v.)(adj.)

In this sentence *is* (a form of *to be,* the most common type of linking verb) connects a noun *(stock)* to an adjective *(worthless)* to complete the characterization: *worthless stock.*

This verb form can also link a noun to its subject:

<u>Tom Bradley</u> <u>is</u> the new <u>president</u> of overstateverything.com.
(subj.)   (l. v.)   (noun)
(The noun *president* is an identification for Tom Bradley. So, the verb *is* conveys no action; it indicates a state of being.)

Note that linking verbs connect only nouns and adjectives back to the subject—not adverbs. So, this sentence would *not* be correct:

The <u>corpse</u> <u>smells</u> <u>badly.</u>
(subj.) (verb) (adv.)

By definition, the adverb *badly* can characterize (modify) only a verb, an adjective or another adverb. Because a corpse has no sense of smell, you can't modify this verb. And there are no adjectives or adverbs to modify. So, this sentence requires an adjective for the linking verb *smelled* (not all linking verbs are *to be* constructions, though they all indicate a state of being), as in:

The <u>corpse</u> <u>smells</u> <u>bad.</u>
(subj.) (l. v.) (adj.)
(Put another way, the corpse has a bad smell.)

Here are some common linking verbs that are not *to be* constructions:

appear	become	feel	get	grow	look
remain	seem	smell	sound	taste	turn

Some verbs can be used correctly in all three verb forms, which is a good device for understanding the forms' differences:

"I smell a rat here," the mayor told the council.
    verb
(*Smell* is a transitive verb—the direct object *rat* follows it. *Rat* does not describe quality of the subject *I*. Note that the question *what?* is answered.)

The diner told the chef that the pasta smelled like dirty laundry.
                                       verb
(*Smelled* is an intransitive verb; there is no object, just a prepositional phrase following *smelled*, to answer the question *how?*)

Now back to that decomposing body:

The bullet-riddled corpse smelled bad.
                          verb
(*Smelled* is a linking verb—it connects *corpse* to *bad,* noun to adjective. It has no recipient of action, just a description.)

Now that we have examined the form and function of verbs, let's look at several other aspects of them: number, tense, principal parts, voice and mood.

VERB NUMBER

Agreement ensures that the number of the verb (singular or plural) is consistent with the number of the subject of the sentence. (You'll enjoy an extensive discussion of this in Chapter 6.) This can be troublesome because identification of the true subject of the sentence is not always easy. Look at the following sentences, all of which contain agreement errors:

The cause for the three deadly fires have yet to be discovered.
(The true subject is the singular noun *cause;* the subject is not always the closest word to the verb!)

Two thousand bushels are a lot of wheat.
(In some cases units of measurement [tons, liters, bushels] are seen as singular entities.)

Among the many reasons for these two financial collapses are the growing sense of investor distrust.
(The true subject here is the singular noun *sense;* don't be fooled by prepositional phrases!)

More on this soon. For now, remember this simple rule: *A verb must agree with its subject in number.* Your assignment: Find the true subject!

VERB TENSE

We use verbs to reflect time. Verbs change slightly to reflect present, past, future, ongoing action or states of being, as in these examples:

The committee <u>reviews</u> the trade legislation today.
   (present tense)

The committee <u>reviewed</u> the bill yesterday.
   (past tense)

The committee <u>will review</u> the trade bill tomorrow.
   (future tense)

The committee <u>is reviewing</u> the bill in conference room 20.
   (present progressive/present participle)

The committee <u>has reviewed</u> the trade legislation.
   (present perfect/past participle)

There are several more tenses and combinations, but you get the idea. It is important to keep tenses "in step," or parallel. We examine parallel structure in Chapter 6. For now here is an example of a tense shift that creates awkwardness:

Frankie is a dreamer, and no amount of bad news <u>was</u> going to change him.

Next we look at a number of verbs that change more radically than most "normal" or *regular* ones, as we examine principal parts.

PRINCIPAL PARTS OF VERBS

Verbs have four principal parts: the *to* infinitive form to establish its root (as an indicator of the present) and three tenses—past, present participle and past participle. Consider the regular verb *appear:* Its infinitive form is *to appear* (we discuss the infinitive in the section on verbals later in this chapter). If a verb is regular, its past tense and past participle form would have an *-ed* ending, and its present participle form an *-ing* ending. Examples:

The team <u>appear**ed**</u> to lose all its confidence.
   (past tense)

She **has appeared** in 200 consecutive performances.
(past participle)

The playwright **is appearing** to make a major breakthrough.
(present participle)

Our language, however, has many exceptions to this rule (surprise, eh?). The following is a brief list of frequently used irregular verbs; note how the forms change, sometimes dramatically.

Infinitive	Past Tense	Past Participle	Present Participle
to arise	arose	(has) arisen	(is) arising
to begin	began	begun	beginning
to choose	chose	chosen	choosing
to fly	flew	flown	flying
to lay	laid	laid	laying
to lie	lay	lain	lying
to ring	rang	rung	ringing
to rise	rose	risen	rising
to set	set	set	setting
to sit	sat	sat	sitting
to steal	stole	stolen	stealing
to write	wrote	written	writing

See a pattern? When in doubt about a form of a particular verb, consult your trusty dictionary, which usually lists (at least) the past tense and past participle.

THE "VOICE" OF VERBS

Verbs not only convey action, they also have a "voice." We discuss this in Chapter 8. For now be aware that voice can be either active or passive. Active voice has more power. Examples:

The governor <u>vetoed</u> the budget bill.
(Active—action moves from transitive verb to direct object, from *vetoed* to *bill.*)

The budget bill <u>was vetoed</u> this morning.
(Passive—though you can infer that it was the governor who vetoed the bill, the initiator of the action is not disclosed in this sentence form.)

In most cases, we prefer the active voice because it tends to be more clear, more crisp, more complete.

THE "MOOD" OF VERBS

Verbs also have moods. Verbs are *indicative* when they convey a fact or question. They are *imperative* when they issue a command of sorts, and they are *subjunctive* when they convey some information that is actually *contrary to fact.*

We have two more areas to discuss, then we can move on to the rest of the parts of speech in Chapter 4. Let's first look at "false verbs," or verbals.

VERBALS: LOVING TO FOOL YOU

What looks like a verb and seems to act like one but doesn't have the horsepower to drive a sentence? It is the simple noun or adjective (and occasional adverb), but the way it is imbedded in a phrase often suggests a strength it simply doesn't have. To make things even worse, linguists refer to such a construction as a *verbal*—as if it is a first cousin to a verb, which allows it to have a driver's license!

These verbals are classified as gerunds, participles or infinitives. They can be the subject of a sentence; they can be a direct object, or they can modify nouns and pronouns to add description—but they can never, ever, act as a verb.

1. **Gerunds.** These verbals, which always have an *ing* ending, have the feel of action but serve only as the subject or object in a sentence:

Swimming is a healthy, low-impact exercise.
(gerund as subj.)

You can see that *swimming* actually represents an activity, not an action. It cannot carry the requirements of a complete sentence. If you dropped the linking verb *is* from the previous sentence, you would have a *sentence fragment,* in reality just a phrase:

Swimming, a healthy, low-impact exercise.

Now here's a pair of gerunds that serves as the object of a transitive verb:

She really enjoys swimming and weightlifting.
(verb) (gerunds as direct objects)

Remember that *gerunds are always nouns.* They will act in the sentence the same way as nouns (see p. 31). Because the gerund also appears as the present tense of the verb with an *-ing* ending, it is sometimes confused with another verbal, the participle.

2. **Participles.** These verbals have either an *ing* or *ed* ending and are always *adjectives*. As an adjective (see p. 35), the participle generally will modify (give extra meaning to) a noun or a pronoun. Examples:

Hoisting her protest sign high above her head, the
(participle)

demonstrator marched defiantly toward city hall.
(subj.)   (verb)

Hoisting is part of the phrase that adds information about *demonstrator,* the subject of the sentence. In this role *hoisting* modifies a noun. The essential action of this sentence is the subject–verb combination, *demonstrator marched.*

Hoisted above the surf by the powerful thermals, she   guided
(participle)   (subj.)(verb)

her hang glider past the dangerous cliffs.
    (obj.)

Hoisted describes the condition of the subject *she,* a pronoun. As Chapter 5 explains, the introductory words in the previous sentence constitute a participial phrase. You'll see that using an introductory phrase that is too long keeps the reader from the key ingredients in any sentence—the subject and the verb. But we're getting ahead of ourselves!

3. **Infinitives.** These are verbals that are formed by *to* plus (in most cases) the present tense of a verb. Infinitives generally are easy to identify; their place as a part of speech (noun, adjective or adverb), however, is not always so easy to determine. Let's look at three examples:

The candidate needs to win.
   (subj.)   (verb) (infin.)

In this sentence *to win* is a noun, the object of the transitive verb *needs.* The object *to win* answers the question *what?* As an object it works as a noun in this sentence:

"This is the way to win," the candidate told her supporters.
(subj.)(verb) (obj.) (infin.)   (verb)

The infinitive *to win* modifies the noun *way.* A noun's modifier is always an adjective. There are only two verbs in this sentence: *is* and *told.*

The controversial candidate is   desperate to win.
                  (subj.)   (l. v.)(adj.)   (infin.)

To win modifies the adjective *eager,* so by definition the infinitive acts as an adverb. (Remember our discussion about the adjective that follows the linking verb and relates to the noun?) See page 37 for information about adverbs.

These, then, are our three verbals. Remember that a verbal is not a verb. (You can walk like a duck and talk like a duck, but that doesn't mean you're a duck!) Verbals are only nouns, adjectives or adverbs.

A final thought before we wade into the remaining parts of speech in Chapter 4: If you recognize verbs and use them well, you have a powerful tool at your disposal. You are on your way. If you understand that a phrase has no verbs and that clauses do, you are on your way to solid sentence construction. If you know that this one word

Stop!

is not only a verb, but also a complete sentence, and if you agree that

a stop sign swaying in a brisk Midwestern breeze

has no verb and is just a simple phrase, you are ready to move on.

Got it?

Go!

 For online activities, go to the Web site for this book at *http://communication.wadsworth.com/kessler.*

CHAPTER 4

Parts of Speech, Part 2: The Supporting Cast

In our everyday use of language, we rarely think about its complex architecture. We dash off a two-line message at the bottom of a greeting card; we issue a rapid-fire response to an email (sometimes wishing we hadn't); we even craft a three-page memo—often without thinking about the functions of words. We can do this because we think we know what "sounds" right.

We believe, however, that good writers need more than good intuition. Good writers need solid mechanics.

Chapter 3 focused on verbs, and for good reason: Our ideas can't get moving without them. They provide power and force to our expression. But what of the noun? Who (what) will be the actor in a sentence? What of the pronoun? What will provide respite for the noun and add informality? And the adjective? What will provide the color, the description to bring an image to life? What of the conjunction, that suspension bridge for thoughts that need connection? Indeed, the "use categories" that constitute our eight *parts of speech* are the building blocks of our writing.

To understand the parts of speech is to master their function and relationships within a sentence. Consider the following sentences. The parts of speech that are underlined show how they interact:

Marisa   hates   mistakes.
(noun as   (verb, directs (noun, receives action)
subj.)   action)

She   really   hates grammatical mistakes.
(pron.,   (adv.,   (verb) (adj.,   (noun)
substitutes helps   characterizes
for noun   characterize   noun)
Marisa)   verb)

<u>Marisa</u> <u>really</u> <u>hates</u> <u>grammatical</u> <u>mistakes,</u>
(noun) (adv.) (verb) (adj.)   (noun)

<u>but</u> she believes we can learn <u>from</u> them.
(conj., joins   (prep., connects word
two clauses)   or phrase to show a
                                    relationship)

MORE REASONS, PLEASE!

So, how will a solid understanding of the parts of speech help you master the challenges of grammar? Here are several examples:

■ Proper recognition of a verb helps you distinguish a phrase from a clause. As Chapter 5 points out, a phrase, which is an important part of sentence construction, does not contain a verb. Therefore, a construction such as:

the dark, windswept ocean sky

is neither a clause nor a complete sentence; it is a phrase composed of several adjectives and one noun. It has no verb and cannot stand alone. It becomes a clause with the insertion of an "action" word:

The dark, windswept ocean sky <u>warns</u> us of a rainy day.

Now we have a clause and, because this one can stand independently, a complete thought. We have a verb. We have a sentence.

■ Proper identification of a sentence's subject will prevent errors in subject–verb agreement. Not all nouns are subjects of a sentence, and the proximity of a noun to a verb does not determine whether the verb is singular or plural, as in this example:

Her <u>decision</u> about the zoning <u>controversies</u>
     (noun as subj.)   (noun, but not as subj.)

<u>was</u> well-received in the <u>community</u>.
(verb, sing.)   (noun)

Inexperienced writers could be fooled about the plural noun *controversies*, thinking that it might be the subject of the sentence and therefore require a plural verb. The seasoned writer, however, properly notes that *about* is a preposition and that the noun it follows is called the *object of a preposition*. There's a complete explanation of that starting on page 39.

■ Proper recognition of how a pronoun functions in a sentence will help you make the correct selection of subjective or objective case for that pronoun. For example, a decision about the use of *I* or *me* in the following sentence requires an understanding of what prepositions and pronouns do:

This is a great opportunity <u>for</u> you and   <u>me</u>.
                           (prep.,   (pron. in
                           requires obj.) objec. case)

Get the point? These are just a few of the many good examples of why understanding the parts of speech is critical to understanding grammar.

NOUNS

You'll recall (we hope) from elementary school that a noun can be a person, place or thing and that it can appear in many parts of a sentence. All of these words are nouns:

integrity

Senator Phoghorn (also called a proper noun)

dreaming

terrorism

You can see that these are not action words, but clearly they can be the activators or receivers of some action from a verb. Because nouns are such a common component of sentences, they have many roles:

1. As the subject of a sentence:

   <u>Integrity</u> is an elusive trait in business today.

2. As the direct object of a transitive verb:

   The governor named <u>Senator Phoghorn</u> to her newly formed Clarity in Government Committee.

3. As the predicate nominative of a linking verb:

   His favorite pastime is <u>dreaming</u> about donuts.
   (remember the gerund?)

4. As the object of a preposition:

   Your editorial about <u>terrorism</u> was quite compelling.

5. As a possessive or modifier of another noun:

The <u>senator's</u> campaign is in trouble.

You'll find that the recognition and proper use of nouns are helpful in making correct decisions about agreement (Chapter 6) and case (Chapter 7). Did you observe that the verb in the preceding sentence was plural? Do you know why?

PRONOUNS

Like a theatrical understudy, a *pronoun* stands in for a noun. It is also known as a noun substitute. Pronouns add flexibility and variety to a sentence by enabling us to refrain from restating the same noun.

Pronouns can be more confusing to use than nouns, however. Some of the most common grammatical problems relate to the use of pronouns in such areas as case (Chapter 7), antecedent agreement (Chapter 6), possessives (Chapter 7) and the selection of the proper pronoun to introduce a dependent clause (later in this chapter).

So, pay close attention as we review the different types of pronouns: personal, indefinite, relative and interrogative, and demonstrative.

Types of Pronouns

1. **Personal pronoun.** The most common pronoun type, the personal pronoun, takes distinct forms in three cases: nominative (subjective), objective and possessive. Let's review them, from first-person singular to third-person plural:

Nominative	Objective	Possessive
I	me	my/mine
you	you	your/yours
he	him	his
she	her	her/hers
it	it	its
we	us	our/ours
you	you	your/yours
they	them	their/theirs

The personal possessive pronoun often lures an unnecessary apostrophe from the unwary writer. The most common problem involves the *its/it's* pair. Errors in this choice are cropping up more frequently in daily newspaper headlines. Let's look at these two sentences:

The stock market registered <u>its</u> eighth straight loss of the month.
(personal possessive pron., modifies *gain*)

<u>It's</u> time for the stock market to return to normalcy.
(contraction of subj. *it* and l.v. *is*—nothing is being modified)

One reason for the confusion about the use of apostrophes with pronouns as possessives is that the noun *does* use an apostrophe to form its possessive. So whereas *her's, your's* and *our's* are incorrect constructions, the following noun possessives are correct with the apostrophe:

<u>Senator Phoghorn's</u> final filibuster
(proper noun)

<u>stock market's</u> loss
(common noun)

Here's a sentence that will either effectively illustrate this issue or propel you to further confusion (we hope it's the former):

<u>It's</u> evident that the <u>stock market's</u> decline has a great deal to do with
(*It is*)   (possessive noun, needs apostrophe)

<u>its</u> relationship to unethical business practices.
(possessive pron., no apostrophe needed)

Got it? We hope so!

2. **Indefinite pronoun.** Because pronouns such as *anyone, enough, many, most, none* and *several* reveal little if anything about their gender or number, they can cause troublesome subject–verb and antecedent agreement problems. For now try to understand the *sense* of the sentence, so you can properly match subject, verb and *antecedent* (a previous word to which a pronoun refers).

The good news is that only a handful of indefinite pronouns can take either a singular or a plural verb, depending on the sense of the sentence. They include:

all   most   none   some

<u>Most</u> of the coastal village <u>was</u> severely damaged by the storm.

<u>Most</u> of the passengers <u>were</u> rescued from the burning ship.

Some indefinite pronouns, such as *both, few, many* and *several,* are obviously plural:

Many are called, but few are chosen.

Indefinite pronouns such as *anybody* and *somebody* can be vexing when it comes to gender identification—and they can cause awkward writing. So, which of the four choices below is correct? (See p. 167.)

Anybody can cast his ballot for town crier.

Anybody can cast her ballot for town crier.

Anybody can cast his or her ballot for town crier.

Anybody can cast their ballot for town crier.

We prefer the most inclusive (and grammatically correct) choice: *anybody . . . his or her.* A writer also has the option of using the plural throughout, changing *anybody* to *people.*

3. **Relative and interrogative pronouns.** Pronouns such as *that, which* and *who* are easy to recognize, but they can be difficult to use properly. Examine the next four sentences and note the correct choices (underlined):

Who/whom did the grand jury indict?

She is the type of leader that/who commands unwavering loyalty.

The aircraft carrier Stennis, that/which is now heading toward the Persian Gulf, is an intimidating spectacle.

This is one of those pens that/which write/writes upside down.

Using these pronouns correctly requires an understanding of case, antecedent agreement, and restrictive and nonrestrictive clauses. Chapters 7, 6 and 9 respectively, deal with these topics. This, however, is an ideal place to mention a common error with relative pronouns— the use of *that* to avoid a *who/whom* selection:

The police officers that stopped my car were polite but firm.
(The correct pronoun is *who.*)

The candidate that the voters selected has been indicted.
(The correct pronoun is *whom.*)

Who or *whom,* rather than *that,* must be selected when the antecedent (in these cases, *officers* and *candidate*) is human or when it takes on human qualities. In an earlier sentence, the relative pronoun *that* correctly substituted for the noun *pens.*

Note that the relative pronoun *who* has a separate possessive form (remember the *it's/its* issue?). The possessive of *who* is *whose*—not the subject–verb contraction *who's* (*who is*). Consider this sentence:

Alice Franklin, an 89-year-old widow <u>whose</u> purse was snatched this
(possessive)
morning, has found a hero <u>who's</u> determined to make city streets safer.
(who is)

4. **Demonstrative pronoun.** These pronouns are "pointers"—their specificity leaves little room for doubt. They include *this, that, these* and *those.* They can stand alone, as in:

<u>This</u> is exactly the kind of accounting trick that will land you in jail.
(refers to a specific example)

ADJECTIVES

If the verb is the powerful engine of a sentence, the adjective is the sentence's "chrome"—its colorful trim. Together these two parts of speech work to give an image both action and dimension.

Adjectives describe, limit and otherwise qualify nouns and pronouns. They do not modify verbs; that is the realm of the adverb. Adjectives are "picture words"—they enhance the detail of a sentence. Like many aspects of writing, they can also be overused and misapplied. Given their many nuances, adjectives challenge the writer to be on target with meaning and intent. There are two types: descriptive and limiting.

Type of Adjectives

1. **Descriptive.** In adding detail, the descriptive adjective expands the meaning of a sentence and helps set a mood. Consider the differences in these two sentences (adjectives are underlined):

Rescue workers continued their search for hikers feared lost in a cave near the Cathedral National Monument.

<u>Exhausted</u> rescue workers continued their <u>frantic</u> search for the <u>six</u> <u>youthful</u> hikers feared lost in a <u>flooded</u> cave near the Cathedral National Monument.

Which sentence paints a fuller picture?

Careful writers use adjectives carefully. They are concerned more with content than with flashiness. Adjectives, properly employed, don't add glitz or fluff; they provide information to create a more complete picture.

2. **Limiting.** Whereas the descriptive adjective is colorful and artistic, the limiting adjective is more spartan. In blue jeans parlance, if the descriptive adjective is designer label, the limiting adjective is plain pockets. This adjective sets boundaries and qualifies (limits) meaning. Note the use of *six* in the previous example about lost hikers. It limits because it is specific. Here's a related example:

The lost skiers had to hike 15 miles to reach help.
(The number *15* tells us specifically how far the skiers had to hike. Much can be inferred from this, though in this case the writer did not choose to add more descriptive detail, such as *tortuous* or *snow-clogged* miles.)

"This turnover cost us the game," the coach said sadly.
(*This,* which often can be a pronoun, becomes an adjective when it modifies a noun, such as *turnover.* Again, the adjective limits [focuses] the meaning of the sentence. The coach is referring to one specific turnover.)

Do you know any ways to improve your writing?
(Though the boundaries set here in specifying ways are very broad, *any* is seen as a limiting adjective because it provides no description or other helpful context. *Each* and *either* also fit into the category of limiting adjectives.)

Degrees of Adjectives

Many adjectives and adverbs have three forms that show degree, intensity or comparison. For example, the trio of

rich   richer   richest

moves from the *base* level *(rich)* to a *comparative* level *(richer)* and then to the *superlative* level *(richest).* Obviously, at the superlative level no higher comparison can be made.

Most adjectives take either the *-er* or *-est* suffix to indicate degree. Some, however, retain their base form and merely add the adverbs *more* and *most* to show a change in degree:

controversial   more controversial   most controversial

The use of *more* with an adjective in its comparative form, such as *richer,* creates a funny-sounding (and ungrammatical) construction: *more richer* (!). See further discussion of comparatives and superlatives later in this chapter in the section on adverbs.

The Predicate Adjective

An adjective that follows a linking verb is called a *predicate adjective*. It modifies the subject, which would be either a noun or a pronoun:

The company's advertising campaign is offensive.
(complete subj.)   (pred. adj.)
(*Offensive* is a predicate adjective. The verb *is* links the quality of being offensive to the noun *campaign*—hence, an *offensive campaign* [adjective modifying a noun].)

The fire marshal charged that the smoke detectors were defective.
                                                              (pred. adj.)
(Read this linking relationship as *defective detectors*.)

Adjective as Verbals

Two verbals, the participle and the infinitive (see p. 26), can be classified as adjectives. Whereas the participle is always an adjective, the infinitive is an adjective only when it modifies a noun. (An infinitive can also act as a noun or an adverb, depending on its role in a sentence.)

Running with a desperation that trumpeted his fear, the purse-snatcher could not elude his angry pursuers.
(*Running*, a participle, modifies the noun *purse-snatcher*. It acts as a descriptive adjective.)

The senator announced her decision to vote against the trade bill.
(The infinitive *to vote* modifies the noun *decision; to vote* characterizes or helps describe *decision*.)

ADVERBS

Although *adverbs* perform descriptive and limiting functions, their uses in sentences are far more complex. For example, an adverb can do all of the following:

■ Modify a verb

The fire raced feverishly through the bone-dry forest.
(The adverb *feverishly* describes or modifies the verb *raced*; in this type of construction, an adverb often answers the question *how?*)

■ Modify an adjective

My latte is really hot!
(*Really* modifies the predicate adjective *hot;* pardon the pun, but it states a degree.)

■ Modify another adverb

The rock star formerly known as Roadkill took his concert review **very** badly.
(*Very* modifies the adverb *badly*, which together modifies the verb *took*; again, these adverbs answer the question *how?*)

■ Introduce a sentence

Why do fools fall in love?
(*Why* is an interrogative adverb; it modifies the verb *fall*.)

■ Connect two clauses

The jury agreed that the plaintiff was defamed; **however**, it awarded only $1 in damages.
(Because it links two clauses that could stand alone, *however* is called a *conjunctive adverb*.)

Many adverbs end in -*ly*, but don't always count on that for proper identification. Examine a sentence carefully to be sure. *Slow* can be both an adjective and an adverb, depending on how it is used in a sentence, but *slowly* can be only an adverb.

In addition to selecting the most appropriate and descriptive adverbs for a sentence, writers should be concerned about the proper positioning of an adverb. Although an adverb can be moved to provide a change in emphasis, it's a good idea to position the adverb as closely as possible to the word it is supposed to modify. Position alters meaning, as in:

Only I love you.

or

I love you **only**.

Comparatives and Superlatives

An adverb can indicate a comparison between two units; it can also express the highest degree of quality among three or more units.

Here's an example of the adverbial comparative:

Prescription drug prices are rising **faster** than the Consumer Price Index.
(*Comparative:* Two items are being compared, through modification [degree] of the verb *are rising*.)

and its superlative:

Ohio's unemployment rate has risen the <u>fastest</u> of all Midwestern states.
(*Superlative:* There is no higher degree of comparison available.)

Be sure that your meaning is clear when you employ a comparative or superlative. Consider these errors:

High blood pressure is <u>more</u> dangerous than any chronic disease in the world today.
(Besides being an amazingly sweeping (and arguable) statement, this sentence implies that high blood pressure is also more pernicious than itself, because it too is a chronic disease. The last part of the sentence should read *than any <u>other</u> chronic disease in the world today.*)

This is the <u>most</u> unique piece of art I have ever seen.
(Certain words, called *absolutes,* defy comparisons. *Unique,* an absolute, is already a superlative. So are *perfect, excellent, impossible, final* and *supreme.*)

It suffices to say:

This is a <u>unique</u> piece of art.

There's more on this issue in the context of clarity and conciseness in Chapter 11.

PREPOSITIONS

Prepositions are the quiet overachievers of sentence construction, and theirs is an important existence. *Prepositions* work with nouns and pronouns to create phrases and to link these phrases to the rest of a sentence, as in this construction of two prepositional phrases:

The judge sentenced Thompson <u>to the Wycliffe State Penitentiary for the rest of his natural life</u>.

and:

This announcement means a lot <u>to you and me</u>.

Like many other parts of speech, prepositions can have tightly focused meanings. Writers sometimes make the wrong choices with such prepositional pairs as *among/between, beside/besides, beneath/below, because of/ due to* and *on/upon.* Part 2 of this book discusses the differences between these pairs.

The prepositions we most frequently use in our writing include:

at by for from in of on to with

Here is a brief list of the prepositions that we use less frequently (note that some are more than one word):

aboard	along	besides	into	since
about	among	between	like	through
above	around	beyond	near	throughout
according to	as far as	contrary to	next to	toward
across	because of	despite	out of	under
after	before	down	over	until
against	behind	during	past	within
ahead of	beside	inside	per	without

Prepositions link with nouns and pronouns to form *prepositional phrases*, as in *to you and me*. Remember that a pronoun must be in the objective case when it is the object of the preposition (nouns don't have an objective case change). So, it would *not* be correct to write (or say):

Between you and I, this marketing effort won't succeed.

The personal pronoun *I* changes to *me* in the objective case; the sentence should begin with:

Between you and me . . .

The same is true for such phrases as:

according to her   for us   to them

Indeed, prepositional phrases always have objects. The English poet John Donne understood this almost 400 years ago when he wrote:

"never send to know for whom the bell tolls . . ."

For more discussion of case, see Chapter 7.

In addition to proper selection of case, writers should pay attention to subject–verb agreement. Consider this sentence:

Each of these bicycles is custom-made.
(subj.) (prep. phrase) (l.v.)

Some writers are tempted to use a plural verb *are*, thinking that the noun *bicycles* is the subject of the sentence. It's not—*bicycles* is the object of the preposition, and that is the only role it has in this sentence.

Writers should also avoid excessive or unnecessary use of prepositions. Consider this bloated sentence (prepositional phrases underlined):

In the matter of your convention presentation, I think that it was rambling and confusing.

Using these prepositional phrases creates an unnecessary introduction. This sentence is more concise and direct:

I thought your convention presentation was rambling and confusing.

One final point about prepositions, long a part of grammatical lore: What is this business about not ending a sentence with a preposition? If it was good enough for the writer of the hit song "Devil with a Blue Dress On," why can't you end with *with, to* or *on?* We feel the same way about this as we do about cracking open fresh eggs with just one hand: Do it so long as you don't make a mess. Scrambling a sentence to move around a preposition can sometimes be awkward:

This is a sentence up with which a good writer will not put.

You're looking for clarity, right? Isn't that what good writing is all about?

CONJUNCTIONS

Some cynics think that conjunctions are placed in a sentence to make it longer and more complicated—that is, the sentence will become so expansive that it will need a conjunction to bridge it. They are correct about the linking function of a conjunction, but they are off the mark about what kind of sentence is created with it. In fact, a conjunction can maintain rhythm and coherence, in addition to creating needed transitions of thought. Let's examine how conjunctions work in sentences.

Coordinating and Subordinating Conjunctions

In its primary role, a *conjunction* coordinates (balances) clauses and phrases of equal weight. (For an in-depth discussion of clauses and phrases, see Chapter 5.) A *coordinating conjunction* can link two independent clauses, which could stand alone as separate sentences:

County commissioners approved the tax levy proposal, but they postponed a decision on an election date.

A coordinating conjunction can also link simple words and phrases that are combined to show a relationship:

She loves tofu <u>and</u> chocolate.

In a stressful situation, avoid jumping out of the frying pan <u>and</u> into the fire.

The most common coordinating conjunctions are:

and   but   for   nor   or   yet   while

When conjunctions are used to join clauses of unequal weight (that is, one clause clearly takes precedence and can stand by itself if necessary as a complete sentence), they are called *subordinating conjunctions.* They often are used to introduce some material or to provide context or counterpoint to the main part of the sentence:

<u>Unless</u> the negotiators can come to an agreement, the strike will begin at midnight.

I will cancel my appearance <u>unless</u> you can meet my contract demands.

The most common subordinating conjunctions are:

after   although   as   as if   before   how   if   since   so   through   unless   while

Pay careful attention to use of the subordinating conjunction *as if.* Be wary of substitutes; a common error is to use the preposition *like:*

It looks <u>like</u> it will snow today.

Remember that prepositions cannot link a clause—only a phrase or single word. In the previous sentence, a writer has two correct choices:

It looks <u>as if</u> it will snow today.

It looks <u>like</u> snow today.

Correlative Conjunctions

This group of conjunctions, operating in pairs, are called *correlative conjunctions* because they pair words, phrases and clauses to provide balance:

Our vacation was <u>both</u> refreshing <u>and</u> exhausting.

<u>Neither</u> the players <u>nor</u> the coach has met with the media.
(Note: In *either/or* and *neither/nor* constructions, the noun closest to the verb controls the number of the verb, as in *coach has* . . .

The most common correlative conjunctions are:

both . . . and   either . . . or   neither . . . nor   not only . . . but also
whether . . . or

Adverbs That Look Like Conjunctions

Words such as *accordingly, consequently, however, moreover, nevertheless* and *therefore* appear to have linking qualities, but they are really adverbs inserted between two independent clauses to provide transition or a change in flow. For this reason they are called *conjunctive adverbs* (we hope that this label doesn't add to your confusion):

Our meeting lacks a quorum; <u>therefore</u>, we will adjourn until next Friday.

(See page 106 about the use of a semicolon in this type of construction.)

INTERJECTIONS

If a preposition is the most understated part of speech, the *interjection* is the most manic of this group. Also called the *exclamation*, it gives emotion and outburst to a sentence. It frequently stands alone and has its own punctuation mark, the exclamation mark:

Zowie!

Oh my!

<u>Whew!</u> An eight-hour visit with Uncle Ernie and his stamp collection is too much for me.

Note that a sentence may have a concluding exclamation mark while not including an interjection:

<u>Yahoo!</u> We're so thankful this chapter is done!

 For online activities, go to the Web site for this book at
http://communication.wadsworth.com/kessler.

CHAPTER 5

The Sentence

The sentence—from the Latin *sentire,* "to feel"—is at the heart of thinking, speaking and writing, an essential building block of communication. It is words rubbing up against one another to spark ideas and ignite emotions. It is thought made accessible, images made visible. Underneath, it is a logical pattern, a systematic structure that most of us have been using with ease since we were 18 months old.

"Give me that!" "I like this!" "Play with me!"

We *know* sentences. We say them silently to ourselves and out loud to our friends. We write them in emails and letters, in notes stuck on the refrigerator door. But when it comes to studying exactly how sentences are created, it's easy to feel so overwhelmed with definitions, exceptions, rules and regulations that we forget we are already experts.

If you see unfamiliar grammatical terms in this chapter, don't panic. You will be reading about all kinds of sentences: simple, compound, complex, compound–complex, incomplete, run-on, subordinated, oversubordinated. Don't be put off by these descriptors, and don't obsess about them, either. Just think of them as shorthand or code. They are a useful way to explain and categorize word patterns. But that's not the goal of learning these terms. The goal, as always, is good writing—learning to put words together with clarity, precision and grace. Should you find yourself caught up in the categories or puzzling over the patterns, remember that when we investigate the sentence, we are investigating a familiar subject, an old friend.

On, then, to the sentence. A *sentence* is a self-contained grammatical unit that ends with a full-stop punctuation mark (period, question mark or exclamation mark). It must contain a verb and a subject (stated or implied) and it must state a complete thought.

A sentence can be as concise as a single word: *Go. Stop. Wait.* (The subject *you* is implied.) It can be as expansive as a masterfully crafted construction of 100-plus words. Regardless of length, grammatically correct sentences result from the same procedure: the selection, manipulation and coordination of sentence parts.

SENTENCE PARTS

Predicates and Subjects

A sentence can be divided into two parts: the *predicate* and the *subject*.

The *simple predicate* of a sentence is the verb. The *simple subject* is the noun or noun substitute:

The computer crashed.
(simple   (simple
subj.)   pred.)

The *complete predicate* includes the verb plus all its complements and modifiers. The *complete subject* includes the noun or noun substitute and all its complements and modifiers:

The laptop computer crashed repeatedly.
(complete subj.)   (complete pred.)

We can continue to describe and modify both the subject and the predicate parts of the sentence:

The overpriced laptop computer crashed repeatedly, smoking and
(complete subj.)   (complete pred.)

emitting sparks.

In addition to modifiers and descriptive phrases, action verbs can be complemented by direct objects, indirect objects and prepositional phrases—all of which are considered part of the predicate. A *direct object* is any noun or pronoun that answers the question *what?* or *whom?* An *indirect object* tells *to whom* or *for what* that action is done. A *prepositional phrase* is a preposition followed by its object. These complements must be in the objective case. Recognizing them will help you avoid making errors in case:

The computer shredded a diskette.
(noun as dir. obj.)

I gave the <u>computer</u> a <u>whack.</u>
    (noun as   (noun as
    indir. obj.) dir. obj.)

I gave the computer a whack <u>with a 500-page user's manual.</u>
    (prep. phrase)

I placed an emergency call <u>to the technical support guy.</u>
    (prep. phrase)

I placed an emergency call to <u>him.</u>
    (pron. as obj. of prep., objec. case)

The complement of a linking verb is a noun or an adjective describing the subject. These words are also considered part of the predicate:

The computer was a <u>lemon.</u>
    (pred. noun)

I was <u>enraged.</u>
    (pred. adj.)

PHRASES AND CLAUSES

Phrases and clauses are the building blocks of sentences. A *phrase* is a group of related words that lacks both a subject and a predicate. Phrases come in two basic varieties: a *prepositional phrase* (a preposition followed by its object) and a *verbal phrase* (a form of the verb—infinitive, gerund or participle—that does not act as a verb, accompanied by its object or related material).

<u>Despite the efforts of the tech support guy,</u> the computer continued
(prep. phrases)
to malfunction.

His goal was <u>to save</u> whatever was on the hard drive.
    (infin. phrase, acting as a pred. noun)

<u>Smashing the computer</u> was uppermost in my mind.
(gerund phrase, acting as a noun)

<u>Grabbing a wrench from the drawer,</u> I approached the machine
(pres. participial phrase, acting as adj. modifying *I*)
menacingly.

<u>Disturbed by my actions</u>, the tech support guy grabbed the computer
(past participial phrase, acting as adj. modifying *tech support guy*)
and hugged it to his chest.

Recognizing phrases and knowing what functions they perform can help you in at least two ways. First, you will not mistake a phrase, however lengthy or complex, for a sentence. Because a phrase does not include a subject (although it can certainly include a noun or a pronoun) or a predicate, it cannot act as a sentence. What it is, as we will see later in this chapter, is a *fragment*. Second, you will not misplace a participle phrase because you recognize that it modifies a noun and must be placed as close as possible to that noun.

A *clause* is a group of related words that contains a subject and a predicate. An *independent* or *main clause* is a complete sentence:

<u>I</u>   <u>wrested</u> the computer out of his hands.
(subj.) (pred.)

A *dependent* or *subordinate clause*, although it also contains a subject and a predicate, does not express a complete thought. It is not a sentence and cannot stand alone:

After he recovered his balance
(dependent clause)

<u>After he recovered his balance</u>, he stomped out of the room, muttering
(dependent clause linked with main clause)
to himself.

Dependent clauses come in three varieties, according to the function they perform in a sentence. A *noun clause* takes the place of a noun or a noun substitute; an *adjective clause* serves as an adjective; an *adverb clause* acts as an adverb.

<u>That I had overreacted to this latest glitch</u> did not surprise me.
(noun clause) (*It*, a pronoun, can be substituted for the clause.)

The computer, <u>which had previously eaten an essay, two term papers</u>
                    (adj. clause, modifies the noun *computer*)
<u>and a biology project</u>, had to go.

<u>After I finished demolishing the machine</u>, I went to a secondhand store
(adv. clause, modifies the verb by answering *when?*)
and bought a manual typewriter.

Recognizing dependent clauses is important. Not only will you avoid using them as sentences—the fragment error—but you can also learn to use these clauses to add variety to sentence structure.

TYPES OF SENTENCES

Sentences come in four varieties, depending on the number and type of clauses they contain.

Simple Sentences

A *simple sentence* contains one independent clause. The most common construction is subject-verb-object.

<u>Politicians</u> <u>dodge</u> <u>issues</u>.
(subj.)   (verb) (obj.)

We can add modifiers—single words or phrases or a combination of both—but regardless of the number of words, the sentence remains simple if it contains a single clause:

National <u>politicians</u> often <u>dodge</u> controversial <u>issues</u> during reelection
(adj.)   (adv.)   (adj.)   (prep. phrase)
campaigns.

Compound Sentences

A *compound sentence* has two or more independent clauses, each containing a subject and a predicate and each expressing a complete thought. The two complete clauses, equal or nearly equal in importance, are linked (coordinated) by a conjunction and a comma, semicolon or colon. *And, but, or, nor* and *yet* are the conjunctions, sometimes referred to as *coordinating conjunctions:*

<u>The issues are divisive</u>, but   <u>talking about them is crucial to a healthy</u>
(indep. clause)   (conj.) (indep. clause)
society.

<u>The issues are divisive</u>; <u>talking about them is crucial to a healthy society</u>.
(clauses linked by semicolon)

<u>The issues are divisive</u>; but <u>one thing is clear</u>: <u>Talking about them is</u>
(three indep. clauses, linked by semicolon and conj., and colon)
<u>crucial to a healthy society</u>.

Punctuation is probably the most common problem associated with compound sentences. Because the two (or more) clauses are independent—actually complete sentences on their own—they cannot be linked by a comma alone. The comma creates a brief pause that separates phrases or dependent clauses from the core of the sentence. By itself, it is too weak a punctuation mark to separate complete thoughts. A compound sentence needs both a comma and a coordinating conjunction. If you do not want to use a coordinating conjunction, use a semicolon or, occasionally, a colon. For more on punctuation, see "Run-On Sentences" later in this chapter and Chapter 9, which focuses on punctuation.

Complex Sentences

A *complex sentence* contains one independent (main) clause and at least one dependent (subordinate) clause. The subordinate clause depends on the main clause for both meaning and grammatical completion:

When politicians avoid tough issues, voters avoid casting their ballots.
(dep. clause)   (indep. clause)

Voters are apathetic because politicians are spineless.
(indep. clause)   (dep. clause)

In the two preceding complex sentences, conjunctions *(when, because)* introduce the dependent clauses. These words, sometimes called *subordinating conjunctions,* establish the relationship between the two sentence parts. Our language has a variety of such words, each with its own precise meaning. The careful writer chooses the subordinating conjunction that best expresses the specific relationship between the dependent and the independent clauses. For example:

Relationship	Conjunctions
cause and effect	because, due to, as a result of, if
sequence	after, before, during, while
time, place	when, whenever, since, where, until, as long as

A dependent clause can also be subordinated to the main clause by relative pronouns (*who, whom, whose, which* or *that*). Note in the first of the following examples that the main clause can be interrupted by the dependent clause:

The one politician <u>who spoke out on the issues</u> made many enemies.
(dep. clause)

She also made friends <u>whose support and loyalty won her the race.</u>
(dep. clause)

Compound–Complex Sentences

A *compound–complex* sentence contains at least two main clauses and one dependent clause. The construction seems to invite wordiness, but a careful writer will refuse to fall into the trap. Here is a three-clause sentence that works:

<u>After the politician went on record against the issue,</u> <u>the media called</u>
(dep. clause)   (indep. clause)
<u>her "principled,"</u> and <u>campaign contributions poured in</u>.
(indep. clause)

If you find that a compound–complex sentence is out of control—so complicated that readers will lose the thread, so long that broadcasters will gasp for breath—break the sentence into two (or more) parts, being careful to maintain the relationship between subordinate and main thoughts.

A GOOD SENTENCE

You begin by choosing words carefully, respectful of their meanings and aware of their sounds and rhythms. You form the words into clusters and join the clusters with invisible seams. A pattern emerges.

You read it to yourself. It says precisely what you want it to say. It has grammatical unity. The idea is coherent; the statement, concise. You sit back to marvel.

You have written a good sentence.

SENTENCE ERRORS

Perhaps you haven't written a good sentence. Maybe you've fallen prey to one of the following ungrammatical or sluggish constructions: sentence fragment, run-on sentence, oversubordination or dead construction. Don't panic. You can catch this at the editing stage if you know what to look for.

Sentence Fragments

A *fragment*, literally an incomplete piece, is a group of words sheared off from or never attached to the sentence. The group of words may lack a subject, a predicate, a complete thought or any combination of the three. No matter what it lacks, it is not a grammatical sentence and should not stand alone. If you punctuate it as if it were a sentence, you have created a fragment.

Like this one.

Fragments can be single words, brief phrases or lengthy dependent clauses. The number of words is irrelevant. What matters is that the words do not meet the definition of a sentence. A common mistake is to look only for subject and verb and, having found them, to believe that you have written a complete sentence. Remember, a sentence expresses a complete thought.

Although they were award-winning movie producers

contains a subject *(they)* and a verb *(were)* but does not express a complete thought. It is a dependent clause, a fragment.

They were award-winning movie producers.
(complete thought)

Although they were award-winning movie producers, their pictures consistently lost money.
(complete thought)

Now that you know what a fragment is and what it must contain, avoiding or rewriting fragments should not be difficult. First, recognize that it is a fragment. It can be a single word, a phrase or a dependent clause. Now you have three choices: (1) Rewrite the fragment to include all the parts it needs (subject, verb, complete thought); (2) incorporate the fragment into a complete sentence; or (3) add to the fragment, making it a complete sentence. Here's how it works:

Their newest picture was a critical success. But a commercial failure.
(fragment)

Their newest picture was a critical success. Unfortunately, it was also a commerical failure.
(fragment rewritten as a complete thought)

Their newest picture, although a critical success, was a commercial failure.
(sentence rewritten to incorporate fragment)

Their newest picture was a critical success. <u>It was also a commercial failure that cost the studio $23 million.</u>
(addition to fragment forms a complete sentence)

Some accomplished writers will tell you that fragments serve a useful purpose. Advertising copywriters seem to have a particular penchant for fragments. In appropriate instances, to achieve particular effects, certain grammatical rules can be broken—and this is one of them. *Purposeful fragments*—consistent with the subject, the audience and the medium—are a matter of style. *Accidental fragments* are a grammatical error.

Run-On Sentences

A *run-on sentence* doesn't know when to quit. Rushing forward without proper punctuation, this construction may actually include two or three complete sentences. Length is not the issue here. A relatively short sentence, like this one, can be a run-on:

The university canceled final exams, students began a three-day celebration.

This sentence is actually two independent clauses run together with a comma. Using commas to link independent clauses (without the help of a conjunction) almost always results in a run-on sentence. In fact, this comma-splice error is the most common cause of run-on sentences. But if you can recognize an independent clause, and if you understand the limitations of the comma, you can avoid the error.

The most frequently used of all punctuation marks, the comma serves a variety of purposes. But one job a comma rarely performs is creating a long pause between independent clauses. This function is performed by the semicolon, the period or, occasionally, the colon. When you force the comma to do a job for which it was not designed, you create a grammatically incorrect construction.

Rarely, and only with extreme care, a writer might violate the comma-splice rule. When a sentence is composed of two or more brief, parallel clauses, commas might be used:

Be correct, be concise, be coherent.

In certain kinds of writing—literary journalism or a stylish feature story, for example—a writer might purposefully create comma-splice run-ons to achieve a particular effect. But this kind of rule breaking depends on knowing and respecting the rule.

Comma-splice run-ons, in addition to being grammatically incorrect, almost always lack clarity. A comma signals readers that they are reading one continuous idea interrupted by a brief pause (the comma). Readers expect the words following the comma to augment or complement what they have just read. But in a comma-splice run-on, the sense of the sentence (actually two or more complete thoughts) denies the message of the comma. There is not one continuous idea. New thoughts are introduced without the benefit of connections between them (for example, *but, and* or *or*).

You can correct a run-on sentence in four ways:

1. Change the run-on sentence to two (or more) complete sentences by adding periods and capital letters:

   The university canceled final exams. Students began a three-day celebration.

2. If there is a close and equal relationship between the two (or more) complete thoughts (clauses) in the run-on, insert a semicolon between them to express this relationship. A semicolon shows this connection and allows the reader to move swiftly from the first sentence to the second. But semicolons are somewhat formal and a little stodgy. They may not work in all instances:

   The university canceled final exams; students began a three-day celebration.

3. In a comma-splice run-on, connect the two sentences with a coordinating conjunction if the two parts are of equal weight. Use *and, but, or, nor, yet* or *so* according to the meaning of the sentence. Always use a comma before the conjunction:

   The university canceled final exams, and students began a three-day celebration.

4. If the relationship between the two (or more) independent clauses is such that one clause depends on the other, rewrite the "dependent" sentence as a clause and place it in front of or after the main clause. Choose a subordinating conjunction that expresses the nature of the relationship and place it appropriately. Subordinating conjunctions include *after, because, while, when, where, since, if* and *although*.

   <u>After</u> the university canceled final exams, students began a three-day celebration.

   Students began a three-day celebration <u>because</u> the university canceled final exams.

Oversubordinated Sentences

Subordination, the fourth way just listed to correct a run-on sentence, is the technique of making one idea less important than, or subordinate to, another. Consider these sentences:

> The Hager brothers co-wrote the surprise summer hit "Fuzzy Little Bunnies."

> The Hager brothers had not talked to each other in three years.

Assuming the idea in the first sentence is the more important one, you can subordinate the idea in the second sentence by creating a dependent clause and attaching it to the main clause.

> Although the Hager brothers had not talked to each other in three years, they co-wrote the surprise summer hit "Fuzzy Little Bunnies."

> The Hager brothers, who had not talked to each other in three years, co-wrote the surprise summer hit "Fuzzy Little Bunnies."

Subordinating one idea to another is a useful sentence-building technique. But beware of oversubordination. A string of dependent clauses, or one excessively long dependent clause, placed before the main sentence can slow the pace. You make your readers or listeners wait too long to get to the important idea, and you risk losing and confusing them.

> After not speaking to each other for three years following the legendary failure of "Mutant Devil Bunnies," despite the efforts of family and friends to bring them together, the Hager brothers co-wrote the surprise summer hit "Fuzzy Little Bunnies."
> (oversubordination)

There are too many ideas here for one sentence. The two subordinate clauses that precede the main idea bog down the sentence and slow the reader's comprehension. The sentence needs to be rewritten, shortening and combining the introductory ideas or giving them a sentence of their own.

> After not speaking to each other for three years following the legendary failure of "Mutant Devil Bunnies," which, although it starred Jennifer Lopez and had the biggest advertising budget ever allotted to a movie in the history of Hollywood, was a commercial failure, the Hager brothers co-wrote the surprise summer hit "Fuzzy Little Bunnies."
> (lengthy introductory clause)

This sentence is sagging under the weight of a 43-word introductory clause that takes the reader in so many directions that the idea of the main clause is lost. To solve the problem, the introductory clause can be shortened or it can become a sentence (or two) of its own.

Another kind of oversubordination occurs when several dependent clauses are tacked on to the end of the main clause. The result is a confusing succession of modifiers:

> The Hager brothers, who had not talked to each other in three years, co-wrote the surprise summer hit "Fuzzy Little Bunnies," which was filmed on location in Akron, Ohio, after negotiations with the city of Newark broke down following a dispute between the production crew and local restaurateurs.

This sentence never seems to end, with a parade of phrases and clauses following the main idea. All these ideas confuse the reader and dilute meaning. Once again, there is too much here for a single sentence. The solution is to rewrite it as several sentences.

Sentences can also suffer from oversubordination when a main clause is sandwiched between two dependent clauses. The result is often an awkward, choppy sentence:

> Although the Hager brothers had not talked to each other in three years, they co-wrote the surprise summer hit "Fuzzy Little Bunnies," which brought them international acclaim but served only to exacerbate their sibling rivalry.
> (front and back subordination)

In this sentence it would help to shorten the phrase *which brought them international acclaim* to *internationally acclaimed* and use it to modify *"Fuzzy Little Bunnies."* But you are still stuck with an awkward, tacked-on final phrase. Two sentences would be best.

Dead Constructions

Perhaps they are holdovers from term paper writing style, but these constructions have a limited place in good writing: *it is* and *there is*. In most cases these words, called *expletives*, merely take up space, performing no function in the sentence. They not only add clutter but also often rob the sentence of its power by shifting emphasis from what could be a strong verb to a weaker construction—a linking verb (*is, was* and other forms of *to be*):

> There was a protest by minimum-wage teen-age workers in front of the
> (verb potential)
> new Monster Burger yesterday.

Minimum-wage teen-age workers <u>protested</u> in front of the new
    (stronger verb)
Monster Burger yesterday.

<u>It was</u> their <u>intention</u> to close down the restaurant.
    (verb potential)

They <u>intended</u> to close down the restaurant.
    (stronger verb)

In addition to strengthening the sentence by using an action verb, avoiding *there is/there are* constructions has another benefit: simpler subject–verb agreement. *There* is not usually a subject. Whether you use *is* or *are* depends on what follows the verb:

There <u>is</u> a <u>bill</u> being debated in the legislature that would increase the minimum wage.

There <u>are</u> <u>plans</u> to fight it.

Looking for the subject after the verb often creates agreement confusion. Avoid both the confusion and the dead construction by restructuring the sentence. For example:

The legislature is debating a bill that would increase the minimum wage.

Local restaurants plan to fight it.

It is/there is constructions are not entirely without value. You might purposefully choose this structure to emphasize the subject and change the meter of the sentence:

It was Monster Burger that led the fight against the new minimum-wage bill.
(emphasis)

Monster Burger led the fight against the new minimum-wage bill.
(no emphasis)

A good rule to follow is this: If *it is/there is* merely takes up space in the sentence, restructure the sentence. Rescue the "hidden verb" and avoid agreement problems. If on occasion you want to emphasize the subject, use *it is/there is*, but use it sparingly.

THE LEAD SENTENCE

The first sentence is important to all writers, whether they are writing news stories or crafting novels, penning poetry or composing ad copy. Competing for a reader's, viewer's or listener's time and attention is serious business. It is here, with the first sentence, that you make—or fail to make—the connection with the audience. You must start off strong.

In a traditional news story or press release for print or broadcast, the first sentence is designed to give the audience a concise, comprehensive summary of the most important elements of the story. Although other forms of media writing, such as feature stories and advertising copywriting, do not require this summary lead approach, they too demand that the writer have a clear sense of what is new or interesting about the material. This ability to recognize the essence of the material is central to writing a strong lead sentence. Combining this ability (learned, with time and practice) with your language skills will help you craft the important first sentence.

You must be cautious because, with its admonishments to tell everything (who? what? when? where? how?) in one sentence, the summary lead approach can open the door to bad writing. Packing a sentence with all this material increases the chance that you will write a muddled, rambling or otherwise awkward sentence. Run-ons and oversubordination are common problems because you have so much information to include:

State lawmakers failed to resolve a budget-balancing stalemate, they worked all week but had to recess for the weekend late Friday night.
(run-on)

After failing to resolve a budget-balancing stalemate, even though they worked all week, state lawmakers recessed for the weekend late Friday night.
(oversubordination)

After failing all week to resolve the budget-balancing stalemate, state lawmakers recessed for the weekend late Friday night.
(improved)

Writing a simple lead sentence with subject-verb-object construction is sometimes difficult because of the amount of information you must include. Remember that compound and complex sentences, if constructed economically, can be both clear and concise:

Food prices rose 2 percent, but transportation costs remained stable, according to figures released yesterday by the federal government.
(compound lead sentence)

The local school board voted last night to allow the distribution of birth control information in district high schools after health officials presented disturbing new data on teen-age pregnancy. (complex lead sentence)

In non-news writing, the lead sentence is often meant to grab attention and pull the reader or listener into the message. Crisp, dynamic sentences are the key, as in this simple but powerful two-sentence feature lead for a story on Atlantic City land speculation:

The most important game in this town is not craps, or blackjack, or roulette. It is real estate, and nobody plays it better than Resorts International.

Consider this attention-grabbing lead that introduces an eight-page advertising insert for the famous M. D. Anderson Cancer Center at the University of Texas:

Everything causes cancer.

Of course, all sentences should be constructed grammatically, powerfully and gracefully. The lead, however, deserves your special attention.

 For online activities, go to the Web site for this book at *http://communication.wadsworth.com/kessler.*

CHAPTER 6

Agreement:
Harmony 100, Disorder 0

There *is* order in the grammatical universe—and writers everywhere should be grateful.

Our sentences are governed not by an authoritarian regime but rather by a harmony born of common sense. Yes, there are rules, but the good news is that they all help us create more effective communication.

It's not always easy. Consider the challenges imbedded in our rules of agreement:

- Find the real subject (it may be buried).

- Figure out which words take on singular or plural meanings—or either, depending on meaning or location.

- Do your genealogy homework and discover the true antecedent of a pronoun looking for the correct verb.

- Stay parallel. Don't lose your rhythm.

Many writers have their eyes and ears "tuned" and realize when something "just doesn't seem right." But this detection system works well only with simple constructions. For example, we all would recognize this subject–verb agreement error:

A huge <u>sell-off</u> <u>are crushing</u> the stock market this morning.
　　　 (subj.)　(verb)

As sentences get longer, however, choices get tougher. How many writers would catch the following error?

One of the nation's largest investor sell-offs <u>are hitting</u> the stock market hard today.

Like many aspects of our grammar, agreement choices are not always clear and straightforward:

A <u>number</u> of rules <u>are</u> easy to follow, and <u>none</u> <u>is</u> without logic.
(subj.)   (verb)   (subj.) (verb)

So, let's pair correctness with harmony as we explore these areas of agreement:

■ Subject–verb

■ Pronoun reference

■ Tense agreement

■ Parallel structure

SUBJECT–VERB AGREEMENT

Consider this seemingly straightforward rule:

▶ **A verb must agree with the intended number of its subject.**

Following this rule involves two steps:

1. Identifying the real (or true) subject.

2. Deciding whether that subject is singular or plural.

The first step is relatively easy, but the second has tripped up even the most seasoned writer. Let's focus first on what a subject is *not:*

■ It is *not* the object of a preposition.

Somewhere between these two <u>arguments</u>   <u>lies</u> the <u>truth</u>.
                        (obj. of prep.) (verb) (subj.)

(The real subject is *truth. Arguments,* the object of the preposition *between,* is plural; though it is physically close to the verb, it has no effect on the verb's number. So, you can read this sentence as *The real truth lies somewhere between these two arguments.*

■ It is *not* a predicate nominative.

The hidden <u>surprise</u> physicians fear most <u>is</u> rapidly growing <u>infections</u>.
        (subj.)   (l.v.)   (pred. nom.)

Admittedly, this is a somewhat complicated sentence. Still it is a good example of how a writer needs to "parse" a sentence to properly connect a subject to its verb. Keep in mind that a predicate nominative, though linked to the subject, does *not* control the number of the verb. In this sentence there are actually two clauses, each with its own subject and verb:

<u>surprise</u> <u>is</u> infections

<u>physicians</u> <u>fear</u> most

■ It is *not* the object of a gerund.

<u>Creating</u> new investment opportunities <u>is</u> her number one goal.
(gerund as subj.)   (verb)

(*Creating*, a gerund, is the real subject. *Creating* is an act, not an action, so it is not a verb. [Remember our discussion on p. 25?] *Opportunities*, the gerund's object, cannot influence the verb's number.)

■ It is *not* the expletive *there* or *here*.

<u>There</u> <u>have been</u> more than 100 <u>cases</u> of influenza <u>reported</u> this week.
(expl.) (verb)   (subj.)   (part of verb)
(Arguably, this sentence could be much more direct, as in "*More than 100 cases of influenza have been reported this week.*" There are occasions, however, when use of an expletive works well in a sentence.)

■ It is *not* a phrase that is parenthetical to the true subject.

The welfare <u>legislation</u>, <u>as well as two resolutions on medical aid</u>,
            (subj.)   (parenthetical phrase)

<u>was sent</u> to the subcommittee for hearings.
(verb)

Phrases such as *along with* and *as well as* merely modify the real subject of a sentence. They do not turn that subject into compound, or plural, construction.

To recap this discussion of "false subjects," here is a list of correct subject–verb combinations (both sentence parts are underlined):

The <u>rate</u> of homicides <u>is dropping</u>.
    (subj.)   (verb)

Her biggest <u>motivation</u> <u>was</u> <u>the children</u>, who grasped hope with
            (subj.)   (l.v.)(pred. nom.)

eager hands.

<u>Creating</u> prize-winning commercials <u>was</u> Dan's lifelong dream.
(subj.)   (verb)

<u>Here</u> <u>are</u> the <u>announcements</u> on the president's agenda.
(expl.)(verb) (subj.)

The <u>fitness center</u>, along with the espresso and wine bars,
   (subj.)
<u>was destroyed</u> in the fire.
(verb)

Now that we have focused on what a subject *is not*, let's examine just what a subject *is*. You will recall from the discussion of sentences in Chapter 5 that the subject is often the starting point of a sentence. Most often it is a noun or a pronoun and it is generally a person, place or thing. It usually appears before the verb, and although it may follow the verb in certain constructions, it is directly connected to the verb in creating action or in being acted upon.

Identifying whether the subject of a sentence is singular or plural sometimes requires thought. Let's examine this area in three ways: (1) when the subject is always singular, (2) when the subject is always plural and (3) when it could be both.

The Always-Singular Subject

This area features several firm rules that should give you little trouble.

▶ **As the subject of a sentence, the pronouns *each, either, anyone, everyone, much, no one, nothing* and *someone* always take singular verbs.**

<u>Each</u> of his stock picks <u>has</u> lost money this week.

<u>Everyone</u> <u>is</u> ready to play bingo.

▶ **When *each, either, every* or *neither* is used as an adjective, the noun it modifies always takes a singular verb.**

<u>Every jar</u> of pickles <u>was</u> spoiled.

<u>Neither choice</u> <u>seems</u> very attractive.

▶ **The personal pronoun *it*, used as the subject of a sentence, always takes a singular verb.**

As President Harding said, <u>it wasn't</u> his enemies who brought him down; <u>it was</u> his friends.

▶ When *the number* is the subject of a sentence, it always takes a singular verb, no matter the number of the noun in the prepositional phrase.

The <u>number</u> of skateboarding injuries <u>has</u> dropped dramatically.

Note that the article *the* is more definite than the article *a*. *The number* implies an organized unit. *A number* refers to an undefined amount; we don't know how many, but we do know that it is more than one. Therefore, this sentence would be correct:

A <u>number</u> of angry stockholders <u>were protesting</u> at the headquarters of Dewy, Cheetum and Howe this morning.

▶ Subjects that stand for definable units of money, measurement, time, organization, food and medical problems always take singular verbs.

<u>One hundred thousand dollars was</u> the winning bid for the abandoned brewery.

<u>Twenty-six miles, 385 yards is</u> the official distance for the marathon.

<u>Six hours of swimming has</u> turned him into a giant prune.

<u>The United Steelworkers has</u> threatened to strike.

<u>Grits and collard greens is</u> a dish I associate with my college roommate.

<u>Measles wears</u> down parents as well as children.

▶ A singular subject followed by such phrases as *together with* and *as well as* always takes a singular verb, because those phrases are merely a modification of their subjects.

The new <u>Internet service company</u>, as well as two of its proposed new business plans, <u>has</u> attracted the attention of venture capitalists.
(In truth, many *together with* and *as well as* constructions can be awkward. There could be more direct ways to say the same thing.)

▶ When all parts of a compound subject are singular and refer to the same person or thing, the verb is always singular.

The <u>president</u> and <u>board chair is</u> Sarah Foster.
(compound subj.)   (verb)

The Always-Plural Subject

▶ **When a compound subject is joined by the conjunction *and*, it always takes a plural verb if the subjects refer to different persons or things and if the subject cannot be considered a unit.**

<u>Two partridges</u> and <u>one pear tree</u> <u>were discovered</u> on the twelfth day of the excavation.
(Note that although the part of the compound subject closer to the verb is singular, the entire subject still takes a plural verb. The rule is different, however, for *or, neither . . . nor* and *either . . . or* constructions, as you will see in the next part of this section.)

▶ **As the subject of a sentence, indefinite pronouns such as *both, few, many* and *several* always take a plural verb.**

<u>Many</u> <u>are</u> cold, but <u>few</u> <u>are</u> frozen.

▶ **Well-recognized foreign plurals require plural verbs if they do not denote a unit.**

The news <u>media</u> <u>are</u> under attack for <u>their</u> coverage of the "Bingo-gate" scandal.
(The singular of the Latin plural *media* is *medium*. Note also the use of the plural possessive pronoun *their* to provide consistency in antecedent selection.)

Her upper <u>vertebrae</u> were crushed in the accident.
(The singular of the Latin-derived *vertebrae* is *vertebra*.)

▶ **A *number* as the subject takes a plural verb because it does not denote a cohesive unit.**

<u>A number</u> of prominent accountants <u>have been arrested</u>.
(subj.)   (verb)

The Singular or Plural Subject

Our language contains a series of agreement exceptions that seem confusing at first. Certainly, this first rule needs some getting used to:

▶ **When a compound subject contains the conjunction *or* or *but* or contains an *either . . . or* or *neither . . . nor* correlative, the subject closest to the verb determines the number of the verb.**

The <u>nose rings</u> or the <u>eyebrow stud</u> <u>has</u> to be removed.
(pl. subj.)   (sing. subj.)   (sing. verb)

Neither <u>he</u> nor his <u>partners</u> <u>have reported</u> for work.
(sing. subj.)(pl. subj.)(pl. verb)

If you must use a correlative conjunction, consider placing the plural subject closest to the verb. Changing the preceding sentence to *Neither his partners nor he has . . .* may be correct but it sounds awkward.

▶ **Depending on their meaning in a sentence, collective nouns and certain words that are plural in form may take a singular or a plural verb. Once again the test of a unit can be applied. If a word indicates that persons or things are working together as an identifiable unit, it takes a singular verb.**

Here are some examples of the proper use of the singular verb. We'll follow each example with a plural use when appropriate:

Politics <u>is</u> a topic to avoid at parties.

But note:

The mayor's <u>politics</u> <u>are</u> offensive.
("Practiced political principles" is the meaning here, not the concept of "politics." If you think of this politician as spreading offensive political practices, the meaning becomes more clear.)

The jury <u>looks</u> concerned.

But note:

The jury were polled on the split verdict.
(Because the jurors weren't unanimous in their findings, they now are being considered individually.)

If you are convinced that a plural verb is required with a collective noun but it just doesn't look right to you (the previous sentence does sound awkward), consider a rewrite, such as:

The <u>jurors</u> <u>were polled</u> on the split verdict.

Acoustics <u>is</u> the scientific study of sound.

But note:

The <u>acoustics</u> in this auditorium <u>are</u> terrible.

▶ Pronouns such as *any, none* and *some* and nouns such as *all* and *most* take singular verbs if they refer to a unit or a general quantity. They take plural verbs if they refer to amount or individuals.

All of the ceramics plant was destroyed.
(general)

All of the theater receipts are missing.
(amount)

Most of the day's work was wasted.
(general)

Most of the team members were uninjured.
(amount)

None of the prosecution witnesses is expected to testify today.
(In this sense, *none* means "not one.")

None of the stolen goods were recovered.
(number)
(The sentence cannot mean that no one good was recovered; it means that "no goods were recovered.")

None is a particularly maddening pronoun, and its use causes a great deal of debate. We believe that the word *none* ("not one") is almost always singular. In the following sentence, however, a writer's selection of plural predicate nominative *(women)* makes the intended number of *none* clear:

None of the indicted stockbrokers are women.

▶ When a subject is a fraction, or when it is a word such as *half, part, plenty* and *rest,* its intended number is suggested by the object of the preposition that follows it.

Three-fourths of Iowa farmland is under water this morning.
(subj.)   (obj. of prep.) (verb)

Three-fourths of payroll checks have been lost.
(subj.)   (obj. of prep.) (verb)

Half of the rent money   is missing.
(subj.)   (obj. of prep.)(verb)

Half of the rent receipts are missing.
(subj.)   (obj. of prep.)(verb)

PRONOUN REFERENCE: THE ANTECEDENT SEARCH

As noun substitutes, pronouns offer a certain economy to sentences. They can also confuse its meaning. Because a pronoun requires an *antecedent* (a noun to which the pronoun refers), its link to the antecedent is critical. To whom do you think *she* refers in the following sentence?

Just seconds after the officer told the reporter and the photographer to get out of the line of fire, she dashed to her car radio.

To employ the classic line of actor Clint Eastwood, "Are you feeling lucky today? Are you?" In this example you may think it's logical that *she* refers to the officer, who appears to be the main actor in this sentence. Logic and clarity don't always rule the day in writing, however. Without a clear connection between pronoun and antecedent, the focus of a sentence softens. If your readers search in vain for a clear reference for the pronoun, you have engaged in a false economy. It's time to rewrite:

Just seconds after Officer McCarthy told the reporter and the photographer to get out of the line of fire, the reporter dashed to her car radio.

A more difficult problem with pronouns is number and person agreement with antecedents. Consider these sentences:

Carrot Top is one of the funniest graduate students who
                   (ant.)   (rel. pron.)
have ever attended this university.
(verb)

(Many graduate students figure in this assessment. Carrot Top is *among* the funniest; he does not stand alone. The writer is referring to a number of funny students who have attended the university; hence the plural verb is correct. Objects of prepositions can be antecedents; those objects are most often nouns, and a relative pronoun can substitute for them.)

Frigid Fjord is the only brand of sardines that   has not given me
                 (ant.)   (rel. pron.)(sing. verb)
heartburn.
(Obviously, there are many brands of sardines, but only one has not caused heartburn.)

The sales manager's presentation was flashy, but not many buyers
                   (ant.)
were swayed by it.
       (pron.)

(You should not be fooled by the possessive *manager's*. Obviously, it modified *presentation*. Most likely the buyers weren't impressed by the manager either!)

Neither of the men had his sentence reduced.
(subj.)   (pron.)
(As you recall, *neither* takes a singular verb. It follows that a possessive pronoun *(his)* referring to *neither* would stay in the same number.)

Remember: A pronoun agrees with its antecedent in both number and person. Stay consistent and make your references clear.

TENSE AGREEMENT: WHAT TIME IS IT?

In general, verb tenses should agree within a sentence or a paragraph. But it's unreasonable to think that you cannot shift verb tenses in the same sentence or paragraph. In fact, you may *need* to change tenses to show correct sequence and historical context:

Although she was a reserve guard last year, Lizzy now rides the
            (past tense)   (pres. tense)
bench only after her deadly three-pointers have given her team a
                              (pres. perfect tense)
comfortable edge.

This is a correct tense sequence. The two shifts make sense because they permit us to understand a chronology. Words such as *although* and *after* help us shift tense smoothly. That smooth flow, however, does not exist in this sentence:

Billy Bob is a poor basketball player, and no amount of practice
was going to make him any better.

This is a confusing shift. The time-warping verbs cause the reader to lose a sense of chronology.

In journalistic style, much reporting is done in the past tense. For the sake of immediacy, however, many headlines are written in the present tense. This is sometimes referred to as the *historical present:*

Headline: Forest Fires Threaten Resort Community

LOS ANGELES—Spurred on by high winds and low humidity, three separate fires in the Angeles National Forest grew to more than 20,000 acres and threatened the luxury resort community of Peach Blossom.

Many news writers use the historical present to create an effect of immediacy or to show that an event, statement or condition is ongoing. The present tense often appears in the lead paragraph, then the writer shifts to the past tense as the story continues:

WASHINGTON—The president <u>says</u> he will not be moved.

At a press conference today in the Rose Garden, he <u>threatened</u> to veto a Senate bill that would slash defense spending.

Direct quotes don't always work well with the historical present. Even though the tense of the quotation should be preserved, its report should not. This looks (and sounds) odd:

"I will not be moved," the president <u>says</u>.

In this case it would be better to make consistent use of the past tense:

"I will not be moved," the president <u>said</u>. "I will fight for a responsible defense budget," he <u>promised</u>.

Another example of the historical present typically occurs in accident stories. The change in tense in the second paragraph is correct and logical:

One woman <u>was killed</u> and three others <u>were injured</u> Tuesday night when their sports car <u>skidded</u> on icy roads on U.S. Highway 20 at Santiam Pass and collided with a log truck.

Dead <u>is</u> Sarah Jane Ridgeway, 28, of Creswell.

Remember that tense agreement is an attempt to preserve historical sequence and context. Avoid abrupt and illogical changes in tense. Above all, be consistent.

PARALLEL STRUCTURE

Some problems of tense agreement indicate another writing problem: defects in parallel structure. A sentence is considered *parallel* when its various units are in relative balance. When a sentence lacks parallelism, its focus softens and its rhythm falters. Let's examine some of these problems.

Common Errors in Parallelism

1. **Creating a series that is unbalanced and awkward.**

   She enjoys <u>books</u>, <u>videos</u> and <u>surfing</u> the Internet.

Why is this sentence unbalanced? It contains three nouns in a series, but the third noun is a verbal (gerund). It throws off the meter; it lacks parallel structure. This sentence could easily regain its rhythm:

She enjoys <u>reading</u> books, <u>watching</u> videos and <u>surfing</u> the Internet.

In the next problem sentence, an adjective clashes with a noun in a brief series:

The economic recovery plan is <u>comprehensive</u> and of the utmost
                                (adj.)
<u>urgency</u>.
(noun)

Using two adjectives to complement the linking verb makes it parallel:

The economic recovery plan is <u>comprehensive</u> and <u>urgent</u>.
                                (adj.)   (adj.)

Another problem in series construction involves the introduction of a dependent clause that clashes with the direct objects of a simple verb. Such a break startles and confuses the reader:

The terrorism expert gave opinions on airline <u>safety</u>, security <u>screenings</u> and that <u>full inspections of baggage may never be implemented</u>.

Readers would expect a series of short items in such a sentence; to have the writer break away and detail one opinion is awkward, to say the least. It is better to list the series and then, in separate sentences, explain what those opinions are. The sentence reads more smoothly like this:

The terrorism expert gave opinions on airline <u>safety</u>, security <u>screenings</u> and full baggage <u>inspections</u>.

2. **Mixing verbals.**

This is another example of selectively <u>using favorable statistics</u> and then
                                     (gerund phrase)
<u>to write a report</u> around that biased selection.
(infin. phrase)

Here a gerund and an infinitive conflict. The sentence would be parallel if the writer stuck with gerunds:

This is another example of selectively <u>using</u> favorable statistics and <u>writing</u> a report around that biased selection.

Here is another example:

She is a diplomat who enjoys <u>seeking</u> new challenges and <u>to rise</u>
            (gerund)   (infin.)
to the top job in her profession.

Sometimes verbals won't do the job. Why not use two verbs in the same tense and be more direct:

She is a diplomat who <u>seeks</u> new challenges and <u>wants</u> the top job in
          (verb)   (verb)
her profession.

3. Unnecessarily changing voice.

Verbs can have active or passive voices (see Chapter 8). Writers choose a voice according to the need to have the subject perform the action or to have it acted upon. Generally, it is best to be consistent in voice. Shifting voice can disrupt the flow of a construction, as in this example:

The burglars <u>took</u> all the silver and china, but the jewelry and guns
         (active)
<u>were left</u> behind.
(passive)

It is much simpler to stay with one subject:

The <u>burglars</u> <u>took</u> all the silver and china but <u>left</u> the jewelry and guns.
 (subj.) (active)   (active)

4. Unnecessarily changing subjects.

<u>One</u> never should argue with a referee; <u>people</u> should know that by now.

Besides creating a stilted construction with both singular and plural subjects, the writer is also wasting words. The sentence would read better this way:

<u>People</u> should know by now that <u>they</u> shouldn't argue with a referee.

Sexism and Parallel Structure

Although sexism is more of a cultural and ethical issue than a grammatical one, the equal treatment of gender also ensures parallelism in writing. Although sexism and other -*isms* are discussed in depth in Chapter 13, for purposes of this chapter we ask you to consider these examples of sexism in writing and note them as agreement issues.

1. **The use of the generic *he* when referring to a noun of unknown gender.**

   A faculty adviser should be in the best position to judge the progress of <u>his</u> students.

2. **Presumed maleness of certain nouns representing a position or class, even if it appears ludicrous.**

   <u>Elizabeth</u> is the best <u>newsman</u> in the chain.

3. **Demeaning or unequal treatment of the sexes.**

   <u>Wall Street lawyer</u> Harold Smythe and Amanda Johnson, <u>a trim, blue-eyed mother of three</u>, will address the city council tonight.

   The men's basketball team posted its 10th straight win, while the ladies' team <u>hung their ponytails in defeat</u>.

4. **The use of courtesy titles (*Miss, Mrs., Ms.*) for women as an indication of marital status when the only courtesy title available for men (*Mr.*) reflects no such status.**

Parallel structure is one of the main building blocks of sentence clarity. Don't think of it as restrictive or rigid. In fact, parallel structure can give great power and creativity to your work. It can make your writing orderly and easily understood.

Achieving grammatical harmony—whether it is the correct matching of subject and verb or the equal treatment of gender—will bring coherence and order to your writing. Your readers will appreciate that!

For online activities, go to the Web site for this book at
http://communication.wadsworth.com/kessler.

CHAPTER 7

Case: It's All About Relationships

We've already discussed the logic and beauty of sentence construction and the sense of order that comes with grammatical agreement. Now we turn our attention to relationships—a gentle way, we hope, to explain how nouns and pronouns function within a sentence.

These relationships are indicated by *case*, which requires a change in form for pronouns in three instances and for nouns in only one. That sounds pretty manageable, yes?

Let's begin with pronouns, as they are the most nimble players in the game of case. They have three forms: nominative (also known as *subjective*), objective and possessive. Let's use the personal pronoun *he* to illustrate these forms:

- *Nominative*, as the actor or initiator of action:

  He will lead the expedition.

- *Objective*, as the object or receiver of action:

  The committee chose him to lead the expedition.

- *Possessive*, to modify or represent a noun:

  The press applauded his decision to lead the expedition. (modify)

  The expedition leader said the decision to proceed was his. (represent)

  Keep in mind that case affects only these personal pronouns:

  I   you   he/she/it   we   you   they

The relative and interrogative pronoun, *who*, also undergoes case changes.

This all sounds simple enough. But, unfortunately, abuses are common. For example:

Between you and I, this test is a cinch.
(Writer fails to use objective case *me* as object of preposition *between*.)

Her and I are going to the mall today.
(As astonishing as this sounds, the misuse of objective case *her* instead of the nominative *she* to reflect the pronoun's role as subject is not uncommon.)

It's much less complicated for nouns because they change only in their possessive form. Here it's the required use of an *apostrophe* and an *s* that sometimes causes trouble (especially when writers improperly try to affix an *'s* to a pronoun to create a possessive). Here is an example of the correct use of both a noun possessive and the possessive of the pronoun *it:*

The expedition leader's decision will be judged on its merits.

It's easy to make a case for proper use of the nominative, objective and possessive. Let's examine how these cases are used.

NOMINATIVE CASE

When you think of the *nominative case,* think *subject.* The subject of a verb, the complement of a linking verb (p. 21) and an appositive (a word, phrase or clause related to the subject) all are in the nominative case:

Sara is an ambitious executive.
(noun as subj.)

He plunged into the icy waters of the reservoir.
(pron. as subj.)

It was he who called the police.
(pron. in nom. case as complement of l.v.)

We dreamers have to work, too.
(pron. is appositive of subj. *dreamers;* stays in nom. case)

Obviously, the nominative case can be used more than once in a sentence: It can appear in every clause. Here is an example of a compound–complex sentence (see p. 51), with pronouns serving as both a subject and a complement of a linking verb:

We must fight this tyranny at every turn; it is we who must oppose the crown's thievery.

Note that the relative pronoun *who* (in the third clause) refers to *we;* that is why it stays in the nominative case, rather than changing to *whom* (objective) or *whose* (possessive).

Use of Nominative with Linking Verbs

Although use of personal pronouns in the nominative case should give you little trouble, be aware that the nominative case is not always used in certain informal speech. The rule that a complement following a linking verb should be in the nominative case (for example, the grammatically correct *it is I*) is not as entrenched as it might be. In fact, these sentences have been acceptable in colloquial speech for years:

It's me. That's him.

That does not ring true in all such constructions, however. The following sentence might sound stilted, but it is grammatically correct:

It was <u>she</u> who broke the story.

The objective feel of the pronoun that follows the linking verb *was* loses force because *she* is next to the subject of another clause—*who broke the story.* Keep in mind that such a construction is not the paragon of clear, concise writing; it is more direct to say:

<u>She</u> broke the story.

or, for more precision and detail:

Tammy Lutz, fresh out of journalism school, broke the story of the judicial scandal.

In any case, try to separate the rules for informal, colloquial speech from those for formal, permanent writing. Although informal style is creeping into some writing, we suggest that you seek a ruling from your colleagues. We hope that the decision does not fall on the side of inflexible (and awkward) grammar.

Selecting *Who* in Complex Constructions

Although there are similar pressures to make the *who/whom* choice more freewheeling, we believe that writers should be careful in their selections. Most of us have little difficulty recognizing the correct use of *who* when it is the simple subject of a simple clause:

The astronauts, <u>who</u> had trained for this mission for three years, were understandably disappointed about its cancellation.

But when the true subject *who* is separated from its verb, the possibility of case error increases. Note this *incorrect* example:

The adviser <u>whom</u> the president said had leaked the information has resigned.

Whom is not the object of *the president said*. The sentence can be analyzed this way to show why the correct choice is *who:*

The adviser . . . has resigned
(main clause)

who . . . leaked the information
(subordinate clause)

the president said
(parenthetical information to provide attribution)

As you recall from Chapters 5 and 6, you must match the number of the subject to the proper verb. You must also select the right case if the subject is a pronoun:

<u>Who</u> did he say won the race?
(*Who* won the race, he did say.)

Who/whom in Prepositional Phrases

A pronoun in a prepositional phrase normally is in the objective case because it is generally the object of a preposition, as in "for *whom* the bell tolls" or "to *whom* did you wish to speak?" (see p. 40). But there are exceptions.

Sometimes a preposition will be a linking device, much like a conjunction or a relative pronoun. Look to the clause that follows to determine whether the pronoun is acting as subject or object:

The chief promises to meet with <u>whoever</u> has a plan for police reform.

Although the object of a preposition normally takes the objective case, the presence of an entire clause connected to the preposition changes all the rules. All clauses need a subject, either stated or implied. Hence, we use *whoever* in the preceding sentence as the subject of the clause (using *with* as a linking device). The nominative choice is clearer when the sentence is rewritten for analysis:

Whoever has a plan for police reform can meet with the chief.

Here's another example:

He discussed the end of the world with whoever would listen.

Note the two clauses:

He discussed/whoever would listen.

Case in *Than* Clauses

Beware of comparative *than* clauses when selecting case.

He is smarter than I.

Than is frequently a conjunction. As you'll recall, conjunctions connect whole clauses and phrases. Because the second clause in a comparison is sometimes implied, you must mentally complete the thought to determine proper case:

He is smarter than I (am smart).

In this sentence the nominative case *I* is required because that pronoun is the subject of the implied clause.

Than can also be a preposition, however:

There is no better snowboarder than her.

You can see that *than* is not a conjunction here, because in this sentence the comparison ends with *her*. Tacking on *than she is a snowboarder* doesn't make sense because the writer is actually expressing a superlative, not a comparative.

This is yet another example of why good writers must master the parts of speech!

OBJECTIVE CASE

Personal pronouns and the relative and interrogative pronoun *who* also change form when used in the objective case:

	Personal Pronouns	Relative or Interrogative Pronoun
Singular:	me, you, him/her/it	whom
Plural:	us, you, them	whom

The Personal Pronoun in the Objective Case

We use personal pronouns in the objective case in the following ways:

■ As the direct or indirect object of a verb or verbal:

The warden led <u>him</u> to the execution site.
(dir. obj.)

The proud veteran showed <u>her</u> the campaign medals.
(indir. obj.—can be read as *showed to her*)

Showering Tommy and <u>her</u> with gifts turned out to be a big mistake.

Showering Tommy and her with gifts is a gerund phrase (a verbal) that acts as the complete subject of the sentence. *Tommy and her* is the object of the gerund (receives the so-called action of the gerund), however, and therefore must be in the objective case.

■ As the object of a preposition:

<u>Between</u> you and <u>me</u>, this car is a lemon.
(prep.)   (obj. of prep.)

■ As the appositive of any word in the objective case:

She gave the cleaning job to <u>us</u> boys.
(appos.)

Guards dragged <u>us</u> reporters out of the convention hall.
(appos.)

The Proper Use of *Whom*

The relative and interrogative pronoun *who* changes to *whom* in the objective case. The *who/whom* choice is one of the more confusing ones in grammar, but it is easier if you analyze the sentence carefully. Let's look at a few examples:

<u>Whom</u> will <u>you</u> choose to run your campaign?
(dir. obj.) (subj.)

Keep in mind that a direct object doesn't always follow the subject and verb. It can appear before the subject, as in the preceding sentence. To make the *who/whom* choice easier, mentally reorder the sentence as a statement rather than a question:

<u>You</u> will choose <u>whom</u> to run your campaign.

Now consider this complex sentence:

> She is the adviser <u>whom</u>   <u>you</u> chose to run your campaign.
> (dir. obj.)(subj.)

Identifying two subjects, two verbs, one complement and a direct object in this sentence helps avoid the *who/whom* confusion:

> <u>She</u>   <u>is</u> the <u>adviser</u>   <u>you</u>   <u>chose</u> <u>whom</u> to run
> (subj.)(l.v.) (compl.—pred. nom.) (subj.)(verb) (dir. obj.)
> your campaign.

Here's another example:

> <u>The caucus</u> <u>didn't know</u> <u>whom to appoint</u> to the steering committee.
> (subj.)   (verb)   (dir. obj.)

In this case it's simplest to read *whom to appoint* as the entire direct object of this sentence. It is also helpful to know that pronouns in an infinitive phrase almost never take the nominative case *(to appoint whom)*.

A final example for this section:

> Do you know <u>whom to contact</u> in the event of a grammatical crisis?

POSSESSIVE CASE

The *possessive case* should be less troublesome than the nominative and objective. In this discussion we concentrate on three areas: (1) the form and use of pronouns as possessives, (2) nouns as possessives and (3) the misuse of descriptive nouns as possessives.

Form and Use of Possessive Pronouns

Personal pronouns have these possessive forms:

> my, mine, our, ours, your, yours
> his, her, hers, its, their, theirs
>
> Is this <u>my</u> book?
> (modifies noun)
>
> No, it is mine.
> (represents <u>noun</u>)
>
> Is this <u>your</u> book?
> (modifies noun)
>
> No, it is <u>yours</u>.
> (represents noun)

Note that an apostrophe is not needed with the possessive personal pronoun. The following is obviously incorrect:

This book is not <u>your's</u>; <u>its</u> mine.

The correct version is:

This book is not <u>yours</u>; <u>it's</u> mine.

Beware the pitfalls of mistaking *personal* pronouns for pronoun–verb contractions and vice-versa. Some indefinite pronouns, however, such as *anyone, one, everyone, everybody, another* and *someone,* do require apostrophes in the possessive form:

<u>One's</u> reach should exceed her grasp.

This is <u>everyone's</u> problem, believe me.

"Possessing a gerund"

When a personal pronoun modifies a gerund in a sentence, the possessive case is necessary because it shows possession or ownership by the gerund, which you will recall always acts as a noun.

<u>Your</u>   <u>lashing out at co-workers</u> is disturbing.
(pron.)(gerund phrase as subj.)

In this sentence *your* modifies the gerund *lashing out,* which is the subject of the sentence. Because a gerund is a noun, it is proper to use its pronoun in the possessive case. The rule makes sense because nouns are linked with possessive pronouns to show modification.

The who/whose relationship

The relative pronoun *who* also has a possessive form: *whose.* It does not take an apostrophe:

I'm the one <u>whose</u> screenplay has been rejected.

Note that the interrogative pronoun *who* also uses *whose* as its possessive form:

<u>Whose</u> armadillo is this?

In the question format, some writers struggle with the *who's/whose* distinction. Like *it's, who's* is a *contraction*—a compression of two words (in this case, *who is*). It is a subject and a verb, not a possessive. If you can read *to whom* into a sentence with your *whose* selection, you're on the right track.

Whose tofu is this?
(To whom does this tofu belong?)

Who's cooking the tofu tonight?
(Who is cooking the tofu tonight?)

More about contractions

As we've observed, contractions can be troublesome with personal pronouns as well. Some of the most common errors involve misuse of *its/it's*, *your/you're* and *their/they're*.

The stock market fell to its lowest point in five years today.
(possessive)

Analysts think it's likely to continue its plunge.
(contraction of *it* and *is*)

Your ticket for the new musical is at the box office.
(possessive)

You're going to love this new musical!
(contraction of *you* and *are*)

Their plans for base camp did not anticipate the possibility of an
(possessive)
avalanche.

They're ready to set up base camp.
(contraction of *they* and *are*)

You can add the expletive *there* to the *their/they're* confusion.

The junta announced that there would be no elections this year.

There's a moon out tonight.

And, to create a complete package:

They're convinced there are no solutions to their problems.

Nouns as Possessives

When creating possessives for nouns, many writers get confused by the choice between an apostrophe and an apostrophe plus an additional *s*. There are more than a few rules, but they are not difficult. Here are eight simple ones, consistent with wire service style, for forming possessives of singular and plural nouns.

▶ **If a singular noun does not end in *s*, add *'s*.**

the student's dismay

Vin Diesel's latest movie

Old-line grammar books have decreed that nouns ending in *ce, x* or *z* (and carrying an *s* or *sh* sound) should have an apostrophe at the end of the word without an *s*. However, many editors join us in believing that most of these words should take an *'s:*

science's pursuit of data

the fox's den

Hertz's rental rules

Note the exception in the following rule for those possessives that precede a word beginning with *s*.

▶ **If a singular common noun ends in *s*, add *'s* unless the next word begins with *s*. If the next word begins with *s*, add an apostrophe only. (This includes words with *s* and *sh* sounds.)**

the boss's machine

but:

the boss' stronghold

the witness's testimony

but:

the witness' story

science's discoveries

but:

for science' sake

▶ **If a singular proper noun ends in *s*, add an apostrophe only.**

Clinton's legacy

but:

Paris' cuisine

▶ If a noun is plural in form and ends in *s*, add an apostrophe only, even if the intended meaning of the word (such as *mathematics*) is singular.

poems' meanings

politics' scandals

measles' misery

Marine Corps' spirit

▶ If a plural noun does not end in *s*, add *'s*.

children's rights

oxen's yoke

media's mishaps (*media* is the plural of *medium*)

▶ If there is joint possession of a noun, use the correct possessive form for the possessive closest to that noun.

Mutt and Jeff's friendship

her husband and children's trust fund

▶ If there is separate possession of the same noun, use the correct possessive form for each word.

Morrison's and Robbins' novels

Zambia's and Paraguay's governments

▶ In a compound construction, use the correct possessive form for the word closest to the noun. Avoid possessives with compound plurals.

Society of Friends' magazine

father-in-law's intransigence

attorney general's opinion

Descriptive Nouns: No Possession Needed

Rather than use an adjective to modify a noun, writers will couple nouns as a descriptive tool. In these instances the possessive form is not needed because the writer does not want to stress ownership.

Descriptive Nouns	Possessive Nouns
government policy	our government's priorities
wine cellar	wine's bouquet
citizens band radio	citizen's arrest

It may be appropriate to join two nouns for the purposes of description, but it will not always work. Sometimes the attempt results in awkward phrasing:

police report on race harassment

Police, a noun, works smoothly with the other noun, *report*, but you can see the awkwardness with the noun *race* when an available adjective can work much better:

police report on racial harassment

The "reflexive" problem

A *reflexive* pronoun *(himself, herself, itself, myself, ourselves, yourself)* "reflects" a personal pronoun to underscore it, as in this sentence:

Can you picture yourself as a movie star?

Somewhat related to the reflexive is a pronoun used to intensify or emphasize:

I myself wrote this screenplay.

Granted, this seems overdone, but it is grammatically acceptable. The problem occurs when these pronouns are not accompanied by the original personal pronoun in a sentence:

I want to throw a party for my friends and myself.

or:

Tommy and myself are going to the mall.

This is awkward and stilted writing. A quick edit fixes it:

I want to throw a party for my friends and me.

Tommy and I are going to the mall.

We hope you can see how case is connected to agreement—and to harmony. Proper use of case adds clarity to your writing. It reflects a polish, an attention to detail. It's worth the effort.

 For online activities, go to the Web site for this book at *http://communication.wadsworth.com/kessler.*

CHAPTER 8

Passive Voice

Here's a quiz for you: Would you rather have someone call your writing (a) lively, nimble, spry and spirited or (b) listless, stagnant, sluggish and leaden? If you chose *(a)*, read on—this chapter is for you! If you chose *(b)*, well, we know you were just kidding. . . .

The adjectives in *(a)* describe *active* writing—for the purposes of this chapter, *active voice*. The adjectives in *(b)* characterize *passive* writing—or *passive voice*—the enemy of energetic prose.

> Awkwardness is caused when passive voice is used. Power is robbed from sentences, and stiltedness is caused. Strong verbs are weakened.

> When writers use passive voice, they create awkward prose and powerless, stilted sentences with weakened verbs.

Read the first example again. Does the language sound clumsy and unnatural, lifeless and detached? We think so. This is passive-voice construction at work. Now read the second example, with the ideas rewritten in the active voice. If you can recognize the improvement—the leaner construction, the faster pace, the straightforward design, the strong, unencumbered verbs—you know why active voice is *almost always* preferable.

WHAT IS PASSIVE VOICE?

Voice refers to the form of the verb. The subject acts when you use the *active voice* verb form. In the *passive voice*, the person or thing performing the action becomes the object of the sentence; it does not act, but is acted *upon* by the verb:

> The accounting firm juggled the books.
> (active)

The books were juggled by the accounting firm.
(passive)

The books were juggled.
(passive)

In the first sentence, the actor *(accounting firm)* is performing the action *(juggled)* on the recipient *(books)*. In the second sentence, the recipient *(books)* is having the action *(juggled)* performed on it by the actor *(accounting firm)*. The second sentence is an awkward inversion of the first. Look at it this way:

Active Construction

who	did what	to whom
actor	performed action	on recipient
accounting firm	juggled	books

Passive Construction

who	had what done to it	by whom
recipient	acted upon	by actor
books	were juggled	by accounting firm

The third sentence is also in the passive voice. Here the actor—*who* juggled the books—is missing. The recipient *(books)* is being acted upon *(juggled)*, but we do not know by whom.

Unless something else is structurally wrong with a passive-voice sentence, it is not technically a grammatical error. In fact, all three of the examples are grammatically correct. But whereas the first sentence is lean and straightforward, the second is clumsy and stilted. The third does not do the job we expect of a good sentence. It does not tell us all the information.

Some novice writers mistakenly think that the presence of *is, was* or another form of the verb *to be* necessarily signals the passive voice. Although passive-voice construction does use *to be* forms, not all *to be* forms are in the passive voice:

The company treasurer was shifting funds into ghost accounts.
(active)

Here the actor *(treasurer)* performs the action *(shifting).* The order is straightforward: who did what. The *was* does not signal passive voice; it is merely a *helping* or *auxiliary* verb. For this sentence to be in the passive voice, it would have to be constructed like this:

Funds were shifted into ghost accounts (by the company treasurer).
(passive)

Note that *funds*, the recipient of the action, is now the subject of the sentence. The actor, *treasurer*, which was the subject of the first sentence, now appears as the object. The order is inverted; the result is clumsy.

In the following sentence, *was* does signal a passive-voice construction:

His "creative accounting" was discovered.
(passive)

This sentence is passive because *creative accounting* is the recipient of the action, not the one performing the action. The actor, the person responsible for the discovery, is absent from the sentence.

His "creative accounting" was discovered by a 20-year-old college intern.
(passive, actor supplied)

A 20-year-old college intern discovered his "creative accounting."
(active)

Don't try to identify passive voice by the tense of the verb or by the presence of auxiliary verbs. Instead, find the verb and ask: Who or what is performing this action? If the actor (the *who*) is missing, or if the actor is having the action performed on it rather than directly doing the action, the sentence is passive.

Take another look at one of the sentences from the beginning of this chapter:

Awkwardness is caused when passive voice is used.
(Who/what causes awkwardness? Who uses passive voice?)

When writers use passive voice, they create awkward prose.
(Active voice: who does what to whom)

Now that you can identify passive voice, let's consider its major disadvantages.

DISADVANTAGES OF PASSIVE VOICE

1. **Passive voice tends to sap the verb of its power.** Partially, this is because of the presence of an auxiliary verb (a form of the verb *to be*) followed by a preposition (usually *by*). But it is also because

the relationship between action and actor is indirect rather than straightforward:

The company was sued by angry shareholders.
(passive)

Angry shareholders sued the company.
(active)

Passive voice can also bury the real verb of the sentence. Look at what happens to the strong, direct verb *accused* in the following sentences:

The senators accused the accounting firm of criminal behavior.
(active)

Accusations were made by the senators about the criminal behavior of the accounting firm.
(passive)

The passive-voice sentence changes the verb *accused* to the noun *accusations*. The result is stilted construction and a flabby sentence.

2. **Passive voice can make a sentence unnecessarily awkward** by reversing the expected relationship of who did what to whom. Subject-verb-object is almost always the clearest, smoothest construction. It is also the most succinct. Changing the order means adding unnecessary words:

Investigations are being conducted by three Senate committees into the company's bookkeeping irregularities.
(passive, awkward)

Three Senate committees are investigating irregularities in the company's bookkeeping.
(active)

3. **Passive voice creates false formality.** It can make a sentence sound impersonal, bureaucratic and overinflated.

It has been revealed by company insiders that "creative accounting" and bookkeeping irregularities are part of a larger pattern of corporate misbehavior.
(passive, unnecessarily formal)

Company insiders revealed that "creative accounting" and bookkeeping irregularities are part of a larger pattern of corporate misbehavior.
(active)

"Creative accounting" and bookkeeping irregularities are part of a larger pattern of corporate malfeasance, according to company insiders. (active)

The tendency to use passive voice to create formality may come from term paper writing or textbook reading, where such overblown sentences often reside. As a favorite construction of politicians and scientists, passive voice is all around us, but as writers we must strive to communicate simply, directly and unpretentiously.

4. **Passive voice may intentionally or accidentally obscure who or what is responsible for an action.** It can hide the identity of the actor from the audience:

Mistakes were made.

Who made these mistakes? The passive-voice construction masks the identity of the responsible entity, but who or what is responsible for an action may be vital information. It may be the *most* vital information! How are we to understand the real meaning behind this sentence if the actor is obscured? Consider the vastly different implications of the following sentences:

"Mistakes were made," the company president said at his morning press conference.

"I made mistakes," the company president admitted at his morning press conference.

The inclusion of the *who* makes a difference, doesn't it?

CORRECTING PASSIVE VOICE

Unless you have a specific reason to use passive voice (see p. 94), avoid it by constructing or rewriting sentences in the active voice. Remember: In the active voice, the actor performs the action. That doesn't mean that all sentences will be alike. You can vary sentences by placement of phrases and clauses, by length, by internal rhythm, by any number of stylistic decisions.

Correcting passive voice is simple once you recognize the construction. Here's how:

1. Find the verb in the sentence.

2. Ask yourself *who* or *what* is performing the action of the verb. When you do this, you are identifying the actor in the sentence. Keep in mind

that some passive-voice sentences omit the real actor. You may not be able to find the person or thing responsible for the action in the sentence; you may have to add it.

3. Construct the sentence so that the real actor performs the action.

Now let's go through the three steps, beginning with the following passive-voice sentence:

An exposé of the accounting scandal is being written by the young intern who first discovered the bookkeeping irregularities.

1. The verb is *being written.*

2. *Who* performed the action? *Who* is writing? *The intern.* He or she should be the subject of the sentence.

3. Construct the sentence so that the actor performs the action:

The young intern who first discovered the bookkeeping irregularities is writing an exposé of the scandal.

WHEN PASSIVE VOICE IS JUSTIFIED

Because passive-voice construction reverses the order of a sentence from actor-verb-recipient to recipient-verb-actor, it can be a useful and justifiable construction when: (1) the recipient is more important than the actor or (2) the actor is unknown, irrelevant or impossible to identify.

In certain instances, the recipient of the action is more important (in journalism, more *newsworthy*) than the performer of the action:

The company treasurer was indicted on three counts of fraud by a federal grand jury.

The verb is *indicted. Who* indicted? The grand jury. But clearly the object of the indictment—the treasurer—takes precedence in the sentence. It is the newsworthy element. Passive voice is justified here.

The treasurer and his top assistant were arrested this morning after a high-speed chase through the streets of downtown Muncie.

The verb is *arrested. Who* arrested? The sentence does not tell us. The person or persons performing the action in the sentence are missing. But because arrests are almost always made by law enforcement personnel, the actor is far less important than the recipients of the action—the treasurer and his assistant. Passive voice is allowable, even preferable, in this example as well.

Sometimes the *who* or *what* performing the action is unknown or difficult to identify. When the doer cannot be identified, the writer has little choice but to construct a passive-voice sentence. In this case passive voice is appropriate:

The company's offices were burglarized sometime late last night.

The verb is *burglarized*. *Who* or *what* burglarized the offices? The desperate treasurer? A minion of the accounting firm? A trio of 10-year-old girls? The doer of this action is unknown. The recipient of the action—what was burglarized—assumes the prominent place in the sentence.

Occasionally, an expert writer might use passive voice as a stylistic device to create a sense of detachment, a sense that no one is taking responsibility for certain actions, a feeling that actions are out of control or mysterious. Purposefully obscuring or removing prominence from the doer might create suspense. Passive voice as a stylistic element, used conservatively and appropriately, may be useful in essays, short stories, an occasional magazine feature or even advertising copy.

SHIFTING VOICES

Do not change voice from active to passive, or vice versa, within a sentence. This muddled construction shifts focus and confuses the audience. Active voice emphasizes the doer. Passive voice emphasizes the recipient:

The company president expressed concern over the bookkeeping scandal, but the drop in stock prices was not mentioned in his speech yesterday.

The focus of the first part of the sentence is *the company president,* the doer or actor. The focus of the second part of the sentence is *drop in stock prices* (the recipient of the action *was not mentioned*), resulting in a confusing and awkward shift. It adds unnecessary words and robs the second verb, *mentioned,* of its power. The sentence would be stronger and clearer if both parts were in the active voice. This poorly written sentence also illustrates the problem of lack of parallelism, both an agreement issue (see Chapter 6) and an element of style (see Chapter 12). Here's an improvement:

The company president expressed concern over the bookkeeping scandal in yesterday's speech but avoided any mention of the drop in stock prices.

Shifts to the passive are particularly common after an impersonal *one* or *you:*

If you study harder, grades can be improved.

The first part of the sentence is in the active voice. The second part shifts the emphasis from the actor *(you)* to the recipient *(grades)*. Keep both sentence parts in the active voice for clarity:

If you study harder, you can improve your grades.

A FINAL WORD

Active voice creates sharp, clear, vigorous sentence construction. It is straightforward and powerful. Be active—and direct—unless you have a justifiable reason to use passive voice.

 For online activities, go to the Web site for this book at
http://communication.wadsworth.com/kessler.

CHAPTER 9

Punctuation:
Graceful Mechanics

This is, bad punctuation.

And this is; even worse.

This is correct punctuation.

If you approach writing as a craft (and an elegant one at that), you want many helpful tools at your disposal. Punctuation is more than one of them. Both hammer and file, punctuation helps build and shape. It is also brush and polishing cloth; indeed, when you add a period or a comma to a sentence, you apply an artisan's finish to the work, clarifying meaning, emphasizing a point or regulating the flow of thought.

We like what writer Karen Gordon, dancing delightfully through her handbook "The Well-Tempered Sentence," says about punctuation:

What is it, after all, but another way of cutting up time, creating or negating relationships, telling words when to take a rest, when to get on with their relentless stories, when to catch their breath?

The punctuation marks we choose will guide the flow and in some cases the intensity of our words. We can't write without them; we certainly would spoil our creative work if we used them incorrectly.

A quick review:

- A *period* ends a sentence.

- A *comma* creates, at most, a pause.

- A *semicolon* slows the reader down, but it isn't powerful enough to stop the sentence.

- A *colon* announces the following: You're about to read a list, be introduced to a fragment or a sentence, or be given a quotation to read.

- A *dash*—maligned by purists but used frequently in journalism—creates a more abrupt break than the comma.

- *Quotation marks* are dedicated "record keepers." They are used to record speech faithfully, signify book titles and point attention to nicknames, among other things.

- A *hyphen* is well-used in our language. It creates economy by joining modifiers that belong together.

- An *ellipsis* warns us . . . something is missing.

- *Parentheses* (they look like this) are used to add needed information without (we hope) harming sentence rhythm.

- Do you really need an explanation of the *question mark?*

- Of course not! Ditto for the *exclamation mark!*

The apostrophe is discussed in detail in Chapter 7 in the context of possessives and contractions.

Although there are styles and fads in punctuation, we writers must deal with logical, consistent rules. Clarity is at stake. Using punctuation correctly depends on understanding sentence construction. For a review, consult Chapter 5.

PERIOD

As the most terminal of all punctuation marks, the *period* signals the end point of a statement. It makes us stop, not pause. Imagine how confusing sentences (and thoughts) would be without periods:

> The flooding that has devastated eastern Europe threatens to worsen at least 120 people have died in the four-day onslaught of water and mud relief personnel estimate more than 20,000 are homeless
> (We'd label this a champion run-on sentence!)

Because of the need for meter (flow and rhythm) and the need to stop readers before they move from one complete thought to another, we use the period. The period actually has two main uses in writing.

▶ **Use a period to end a sentence that is neither interrogative (?) nor exclamatory (!).**

Coach Thomas asked the umpire whether he'd like to see an ophthalmologist.

▶ **Use a period to create certain abbreviations and to indicate decimals.**

Gov. Adams has vetoed the $58.5 million highway appropriation.

Abbreviations are space savers, and periods help signal these shortcuts. Not all abbreviations, however, require periods. *Acronyms* (abbreviations without punctuation, which are pronounceable words—for example, *UNESCO* and *AIDS*), names of certain organizations and government agencies (*NBC, UAW, FBI* and *CIA*) and abbreviations of technical words (*mph* and *rpm*)—do not require periods. To learn which abbreviations use periods and which ones don't, consult a dictionary or your publication's stylebook.

One other quick note about periods: They always go inside quotation marks or inside an ending parenthesis if the parenthetical information is a complete sentence:

The candidate warned, "You can expect a lot of vetoes if I am elected."

The incumbent has a memorable history of vetoes herself. (She rejected more than 75 bills in the last session, and most of them survived a revote.)

COMMA

The *comma* is used mainly for clarity and meter. Let's examine proper use of the comma and then look at some of its inappropriate uses.

▶ **Use commas to separate items in a series.**

I can't believe that you ate seven hot dogs, two plates of coleslaw, a raw onion and three pieces of pumpkin pie in one sitting.

The forecast calls for light showers, some clearing and morning fog.

The rule that controls the *serial comma* is this: When the last item in a series is connected by a coordinating conjunction (*and, or, but, nor, for, yet, so)*, the comma can be omitted before that conjunction. This is especially true when the series is short or uncomplicated. If the series is longer, however, the comma can be inserted before the conjunction to eliminate confusion:

> Union officials this morning said they would bargain vigorously for the right to negotiate pension fund investments, for an expanded procedure of grievance procedures, and for binding arbitration of all contract matters not settled within 90 days of the start of negotiations.

We should note that the elimination of the serial comma is particularly favored in journalistic writing. It is used more frequently in formal composition, novels and academic texts, and it's not unusual in the teaching of standard English to emphasize use of the serial comma.

▶ **Use a comma to separate two independent clauses connected by a coordinating conjunction, so long as the clauses don't contain much internal punctuation.**

> Volcanic activity persists on the <u>mountain, but</u> park officials will continue to issue climbing permits on a limited basis.

Remember that an independent clause can stand alone as a complete sentence. A compound predicate (two or more verbs that serve the same subject) does not need a comma because it is part of the same clause:

> The <u>judge fined</u> the men $500 and <u>ordered</u> them to perform 40 hours
>   (subj.)(verb #1)   (verb #2)
> of community service.

Journalistic style favors dropping the comma if both independent clauses of the sentence are short and if the sentence does not lose its meter:

> The legislature approved the bill but the governor vetoed it.

When in doubt about these constructions, leave the comma in.

▶ **Use a comma to set off long introductory clauses and phrases and some shorter clauses and phrases that would be confusing without it.**

> When he finally realized he was holding the winning lottery ticket, he calmly left his office and never returned.

> To Tom Hanks, Oscar is a familiar name.

You can omit the comma for some short clauses and phrases if no run-on occurs in the sentence—that is, if the meaning of the introductory segment remains distinct from the rest of the sentence. For example, a comma is not necessary in these sentences:

At dinner we finally declared a truce.

From the darkness came a bloodcurdling howl.

▶ **Use commas to set off nonrestrictive (nonessential) clauses, phrases and modifiers from the rest of the sentence.**

Restrictive (essential)

Clauses, phrases or words that are essential to the meaning of the sentence are called *restrictive*. They need not be set off from the rest of the sentence:

The three men who hijacked a city bus died when they crashed into a police blockade.

The subordinate clause *who hijacked a city bus* limits the meaning of the sentence. One test to determine restrictive meaning is to read the sentence without the clause in question. If you find yourself trying to fill in the meaning of the sentence, that clause is essential. Consider the preceding example:

The three men died when they crashed into a police blockade.

This clearly requires its accompanying clause to make the sentence more complete, more understandable. (What men? What did they do?) For this reason the clause *who hijacked a city bus* should not be set off by commas.

Here's another example:

The ground beef that was labeled with numbers 112 and 114-H has been recalled by state officials.

Not all ground beef has been recalled. Because the subordinate clause *that was labeled . . .* is essential to the meaning of the sentence, no commas should be used.

Note that in a restrictive clause the pronoun *that* is used instead of *which*. If the clause is not essential to the meaning of the sentence but simply provides added detail, use *which* and set off the clause with commas. (See the entry in Part 2 for *that/which/who.*)

Nonrestrictive (nonessential)

Nonrestrictive clauses, phrases and words *require* commas because they are nonessential, or incidental, to the sentence. Notice how these examples differ from the restrictive constructions:

> Edwards, who turns 75 tomorrow, will appear before the parole board to argue that 15 years of a 25-year sentence is sufficient punishment for his robbery conviction.

This sentence does not depend on the underlined subordinate clause to complete its meaning. Other nonessential, amplifying pieces of information could have been added, such as *who has consistently maintained his innocence.*

> Tom's barbeque sauce, which he says is based on his grandmother's recipe, won the blue ribbon at the Hogmaw County Fair.

The subordinate clause about the origin of the recipe is not essential to the meaning of the sentence. It could be eliminated, and an understandable, complete sentence would remain.

> Sam Bradley, the Sioux City spitballer of Boston Braves fame, died last night at 78.

The underlined phrase is called an *appositive*—a word or phrase that further defines the word that precedes it. It is not essential to the sentence but adds greater information and context.

▶ **Use commas to separate descriptive modifiers of equal rank.**

When a noun is preceded by a string of adjectives, apply this two-part test to determine whether those modifiers need to be separated by commas: Can you use these adjectives interchangeably? Can you successfully insert the conjunction *and* between them and have the sentence make sense? If so, these adjectives are coordinate and *require* a comma.

Given this test, the modifiers in the following sentence do *not* need a comma:

Meteorologists forecast another cold Midwestern night.
(The noun *night* has two modifiers—*cold* and *Midwestern.* You can't read "cold *and* Midwestern night" into this construction, so the adjectives need not be separated by a comma.)

When you add a coordinate modifier, however, the punctuation changes:

Meteorologists forecast another <u>cold, dreary</u> Midwestern night.
(You can read "cold *and* dreary" into this sentence. They modify
Midwestern night equally, so they are considered coordinate, and the
comma is necessary.)

This sentence shows the proper use of a comma with coordinate
modifiers:

Stocks rose today in <u>frantic, irrational</u> trading.

▶ **Use commas to set off parenthetical expressions.**

A *parenthetical expression* is similar to a theatrical aside: It is not part of
the main (onstage) conversation but is intended to give extra information
in a quieter tone. These statements could be put in parentheses, but that
might be too formal and stilted. Use commas to create shorter pauses
without disrupting the flow of the sentence:

Could such a game, <u>she asked herself,</u> ever be surpassed?

▶ **Use commas when the absence of a pause can cause confusion.**

<u>For the senator,</u> going fishing for three hours is vacation enough.

<u>Circling the brewery,</u> workers chanted noisily to protest unsafe working
conditions.

It would be a false economy to waive comma use in the preceding two
examples. The pause is necessary for clarity.

▶ **Use commas to set off participial phrases that modify some part of
the independent clause.**

The Senate adjourned today, <u>having defeated an attempt to extend</u>
<u>the session</u>.   (participial phrase modifies *Senate*)

Various stylebooks list many other examples of comma use (and
nonuse). Some may be obvious to you:

1,250 votes—but 999 votes

He lives in Wapakoneta, Ohio.

Ozzie, will you answer the door?

Comma Misuse

What is it about commas that makes some writers want to sprinkle them all over their prose, like sugar on cereal? The comma is designed to improve the flow of prose, not weigh it down, but poor construction and comma overuse often combine to create a form of literary stammering. Writers and editors must be careful to avoid excessive use of the comma. Here are some helpful rules:

▶ **Do not use a comma to separate two independent clauses that are not joined by a coordinating conjunction.**

Violating this rule produces the *comma splice,* one of the most common errors in punctuation. It looks like this:

The unemployment rate continues to drop, the rate of inflation remains constant.

I don't know why you are so insistent about this, it will lead only to more trouble.

Using a comma to link two independent clauses (which could stand alone as separate sentences) does not create an effective break in thought and causes a run-on sentence. We recommend that you either break the sentence in two or do one of the following:

■ Use a semicolon to link the clauses.

The unemployment rate continues to drop; the rate of inflation remains constant.

■ Use a coordinating conjunction with a comma.

The unemployment rate continues to drop, but the rate of inflation remains constant.

▶ **Do not use a comma to introduce a subordinate clause.**

The use of a comma before *because* is one of the biggest offenders. *Because* is a *subordinating conjunction*—it introduces a dependent clause:

The mayor inspected the crash site because she needed a firsthand report.

No comma is needed here because the conjunction does not coordinate equal clauses. (Did you notice the lack of a comma in the previous sentence as well?) That is why *and, but* and *or* often require commas; they are called *coordinating conjunctions* because they link clauses of equal weight. (See "Conjunctions" in Chapter 4 for a list of conjunctions that do not coordinate.)

Note that if the subordinate clause is used at the beginning of the sentence, a comma *is* required:

> Because she needed a firsthand <u>report, the</u> mayor inspected the crash site.

▶ **Do not use a comma to separate a noun or a pronoun from its reflexive.**

A *reflexive* is any of the "self" pronouns *(myself, himself)* used to intensify or accent the noun or pronoun preceding it. A comma is not needed to set off the reflexive:

> Meriwether <u>himself</u> will lead the rescue party.

▶ **Do not use a comma between a word and a phrase that amplifies it if it will create a "false series."**

This sentence, as punctuated, is bound to cause confusion:

> Rescuers discovered seven bodies, four office workers, two firefighters and one police officer.

Unless the writer meant to say that 14 people were discovered and that seven of them were dead, the comma use after *bodies* is wrong. A colon or dash would be more effective in separating the two ideas:

> Rescuers discovered seven bodies—those of four office workers, two firefighters and one police officer.

▶ **Do not use a comma to precede a partial quotation.**

> The mayor says his opponent is "a rat dressed in weasel's clothing."

No comma is needed because the quoted material is the predicate nominative of the verb *is*. Because the quoted material depends on the rest of the sentence for its context, that material should not be set off by a comma.

If the quotation is a full sentence, however, it should be preceded by a comma:

> The public defender asked, "How would you like to be sent to prison for a crime you didn't commit?"

Remember: Good writers use commas for clarity and meter. If your sentences contain a clutter of commas, take heed. Perhaps the sentences are too long and too busy. Be brief; be crisp; be sparing in your use of the comma.

SEMICOLON

The *semicolon* is a curious but effective mark of punctuation: It is half comma, half period. It indicates more than a pause; it is a break but not a stop. It is more inflexible than the comma or the period; it carries a grammatical formality that some writers would just as soon avoid in their work. For this reason, perhaps, the semicolon is used infrequently in news writing.

Writers sometimes opt for two separate and shorter sentences rather than joining two independent clauses with a semicolon. They may choose to break up a series of thoughts normally punctuated by semicolons to avoid long clauses and phrases. Their hesitance to use the semicolon shows their dependence on the period. They equate the "full stop" with simplicity and clarity. The semicolon apparently doesn't project that image, although it is clear that that semicolon can provide a fairly strong break.

Here are three guidelines to help you properly employ the semicolon:

▶ **Use a semicolon to join independent clauses not connected by a coordinating conjunction.**

Sarah will contest the election <u>results; she</u> says she will accept the outcome of a "properly supervised" recount.

If those two clauses had been connected with the coordinating conjunction *but*, a comma would have sufficed:

... election results, but she says she ...

Some writers prefer the use of the coordinating conjunction because it gives more specific direction to the reader. Others would look at these two long clauses and break them into two sentences.

Words like *however, moreover, nevertheless* and *therefore* are not coordinating conjunctions. They are *conjunctive adverbs*. They do not perform the linking function of a conjunction and cannot coordinate clauses of equal rank. When a conjunctive adverb separates two independent clauses, a semicolon is required.

> At 35, Maria Thomas has already achieved more than most of her <u>peers; however</u>, she says she will never be satisfied.

As we mentioned in the "Comma Misuse" section, using a comma here to separate the two clauses would create a comma splice.

Semicolons also are needed when more than two independent clauses are linked in a series—even when the last part of the series is connected by a coordinating conjunction:

> We will find proper funding for our <u>schools; we</u> will not abandon our commitment to greater access to higher <u>education; and</u> we will press for a new income tax measure to fully fund our programs.

▶ **Use a semicolon to separate internally punctuated independent clauses joined by a coordinating conjunction.**

When you punctuate a clause internally with commas, you can't use a comma to separate that clause from another. A semicolon is needed to create a more abrupt stop:

> The city council has approved the proposed levy, which will go to voters in May; but, the mayor has indicated that she will campaign against it.

▶ **Use a semicolon to set off parts of a series that also contain commas.**

> Killed in the early morning collision were Aaron Jepsen, 37, of Brookings; his wife, Rhona, 32; and their children, Tom, 12; Betty, 9; and Richard, 4.

The main function of the semicolon here is organization. It tidies up elements of a series so that they remain distinct.

We believe that the semicolon is helpful when it clarifies boundaries in a series containing commas. But we urge you to avoid using the semicolon to connect two independent clauses, even though it is grammatically correct. If you must use it, be sure that the two clauses actually need some connection and that they wouldn't be better off as separate sentences. For example, don't write:

> The car slid off the narrow roadway into a muddy embankment; police arrived hours later to find that no one had survived.

when you could write:

The car slid off the narrow roadway into a muddy embankment. When police arrived hours later, they found three bodies in the overturned vehicle.

As you can see, merging two strong thoughts into one construction can be economical, but it may not give you the completeness and creativity that two sentences can. Think of the semicolon as a clarifier, not an economizer.

COLON

The *colon* presents ideas with a flourish: It announces. It ushers in complete sentences, lists, quotations and dialogue.

Proper Use of the Colon

When the colon is used to introduce a complete sentence, the first word of that sentence should be capitalized:

> Rock star Dewdrop Boysenberry has a bold idea: He will challenge wrestler Hulk Hogan for a congressional seat.

When a colon is used to introduce a word, phrase or clause that is not a complete sentence, the first word following the colon should *not* be capitalized:

> In the movie classic "The Graduate," Dustin Hoffman learned the one word that would guarantee a successful future: *plastics.*

Here are some other uses of the colon:

▶ **Use a colon to introduce a quotation that is longer than one sentence and to end a paragraph that introduces a quotation in the next paragraph.**

The judge eyed the defendant and told him in words dripping with disdain: "Your disgusting conduct in my courtroom has mocked everything that is justice. Please accept our jail hospitality for the next 45 days."

Here is the text of the president's speech:
"Good evening, my fellow Americans . . ."

▶ **Use colons to show the text of questions and answers.**

This can take two forms:

Q: And then what happened?

A: She put the meat cleaver down and called the cops.

Sneed: Senator, I have done my best to contribute to this discussion.

Ervin: Somebody told me once when I was representing a case; he said, "You put up the best possible case for a guilty client!"

As you can see, the colon eliminates the need for quotation marks unless the dialogue itself quotes other material.

▶ **Use colons to show times and citations.**

She ran the 5,000 meters in 15:02.

Psalm 101:5 tells us of the danger of slander.

When Not to Use the Colon

▶ **You do not need the colon when you are introducing a short list without the words *the following.***

The Dallas Cowboys have drafted Huey, Dewey and Louie.

▶ **You do not need a colon when introducing a direct quotation of one sentence or less. A comma is sufficient.**

What do you think of his comment, "I am not a crook"?

Note the placement of the question mark. If the quoted material is not asking a question, leave the question mark outside the quotation marks.

DASH

What is longer than a hyphen, less formal than a colon, more direct than parentheses—and really *not* the new kid on the punctuation block? It's the *dash* and it's been around quite a while. In formal grammar its primary uses are to change direction and create emphasis. Journalists, on the other hand, can be rightfully accused of using the dash to excess or of using it when a comma, a colon or parentheses might be more skillfully employed. We believe that the dash should be used sparingly because it is a startling mark of punctuation. If used too often, it loses its impact. Let's look at the two main uses of the dash in all writing.

▶ **Use a dash to end a sentence with a surprising or ironic element.**

The tall, distinguished-looking man entered the country with a valid passport, two pieces of leather luggage, an antique Leica camera around his neck—and 16 ounces of uncut heroin in the heels of his alligator boots.

A comma here would not be as effective in changing meter and warning the reader of a break in thought. Using this reasoning you would not want a dash in this less surprising sentence:

Chicago streets are punctuated with classic architecture, historic sites and glitzy stores.

That series contains similar, unsurprising information. Adding a dash would give the sentence false drama.

▶ **Use dashes to set off a long clause or a phrase that is in apposition to the main clause, when it makes the information clearer and more distinctive.**

The closing ceremonies of the Olympics—a dazzling spectacle of unrequited self-promotion—set off an explosion of self-congratulations at the network.

A comma usually suffices with a shorter appositive that does not require an abrupt break:

Baker, the Giants' far-ranging outfielder, silenced his critics with a rifle throw that cut down the speeding Thomas at home plate.

Dashes could also be used to set off both parenthetical expressions and a series of items in the middle of a sentence. We recommend restraint with these uses, however, and that you concentrate on the two main uses of the dash. The dash should be used only infrequently—make sure your reader will take notice of it!

QUOTATION MARKS

Quotation marks have several identities. They can be a tool of truthfulness when they give a faithful reproduction of what was said. They can also be a weapon that belittles. For example, what impressions do quotation marks create in these sentences?

"I believe we can correct this situation," the accountant said.
(This seems to be a straightforward reproduction of what was said.)

The accountant said her firm could correct the "situation."
(Placement of quotation marks around *situation* makes us suspicious.)

What is so strange about this so-called situation? The quotation marks alert us to the possibility of another meaning. Let's look at the appropriate use of quotation marks in writing and then see how other marks of punctuation are used with quotations.

Proper Use of Quotation Marks

▶ **Use quotation marks to enclose direct quotations and dialogue.**

"We must complete construction of our third nuclear plant with all due speed to maintain our high bond rating," Board President Ann Armes said.

"So, did you actually see the gun?" the defense attorney asked.

"No, well, I thought I did," the defendant replied.

"I'll take that as a no."

Avoid the unnecessary use of partial quotations. Sometimes a paraphrase will do. So, instead of:

Board President Ann Armes said completion of a third nuclear plant is necessary "to maintain our high bond rating."

you might write:

Completion of a third nuclear plant is necessary to preserve the board's high bond rating, according to Board President Ann Armes.

The partial quotation works best if the language or style of what is quoted is distinctive or colorful. For example, it would be difficult to paraphrase this effectively:

Sen. Tony Meeker, R-Amity, compared the higher-education system to a dinosaur that's "going to fall in the tar pits and become a fossil."

Avoid putting quotation marks around single words if their use results in an inaccurate representation. We generally put these marks around unfamiliar terms on first reference, around slang words and around words used sarcastically or ironically. But don't overdo it!

A wage freeze is in effect.

His luck ran into a "freeze" at the track.

Tammy Lutz's dreams are a $10 million business.

Tom Anderson's "dreams" have ruined those of elderly investors who spent their life savings on his worthless pyramid scheme.

▶ **Use quotation marks for titles of books, lectures, movies, operas, plays, poems, songs, speeches, television shows and works of art. Do *not* use these marks for names of magazines, newspapers, reference books or the Bible.**

"Jane Eyre"

"The Real Reason for Baldness"

"Austin Powers"

"Il Trovatore"

But note:

The New Yorker

The Portland Oregonian

The Foundation Directory

▶ **Use quotation marks for nicknames.**

John "The Duke" Wayne

"Bad Moon Rising" Davis

Use of Other Punctuation with Quotation Marks

One of the most frequently asked questions about quotation marks involves the placement of other punctuation marks with them. "Does the question mark go inside or outside?" Like so many aspects of grammar, that depends. (Remember, coping with uncertainty makes you stronger!) Here are your guidelines:

Punctuation that goes inside quotation marks

A bit of dogma first:

▶ **The period and comma always go inside quotation marks.**

The defendant replied, "I refuse to answer on the grounds that it may incriminate me."

"I'll wait for you here," she said.

▶ **Question marks and exclamation marks go inside quotation marks if they are part of the quoted material.**

The governor asked, "Do you believe that your quality of life has improved during my administration?"

"Give me my dignity!" the prisoner pleaded.

Punctuation that goes outside quotation marks

▶ **Question marks and exclamation marks go outside if they are not part of the quoted material.**

Have you read "Being Your Own Best Friend"?

Whatever you do, don't see "Slasher Five"!

HYPHEN

Whereas the dash sets words apart, the *hyphen* brings them together. It is a tiny bridge that links words to indicate compound constructions and modifiers. Unfortunately, the hyphen can be as frustrating as it is useful. If you use it to join words that need to work as a unit, and if you use it to avoid confusion, the hyphen will serve you well.

▶ **Use a hyphen to join compound modifiers that precede a noun unless that modifier is preceded by *very* or an *-ly* adverb.**

Compound modifiers belong together. They are not part of a series of adjectives and adverbs that can separately describe the word they are modifying. The components of a compound modifier actually modify themselves as they describe the noun:

a <u>fair-weather</u> friend
(This is a compound modifier. *Fair* doesn't modify *friend*. It modifies the other modifier, *weather*. Together they modify *friend*. The friend is fair-weathered, not fair and weather, so we use the hyphen.)

a <u>sluggish, unresponsive</u> economy
(This is not a compound modifier. The economy is both sluggish and unresponsive. *Sluggish* doesn't modify *unresponsive*. No hyphen is needed.)

If you can insert the conjunction *and* between the modifiers and make sense of the new construction, you do not have a compound modifier. A *sluggish and unresponsive economy* sounds right, but a *fair and weather friend* does not. That should be your signal for a hyphen under this rule, unless the beginning of the compound modifier is *very* or an *-ly* adverb. These words are a clear signal to the reader that a compound modifier is coming. No hyphen is needed in these cases:

<u>very wealthy</u> investor

<u>heavily spiced</u> recipe

Most compound modifiers are also hyphenated when they follow a form of the linking verb *to be*. In that sense they continue to modify the subject. So, it is proper to write:

She is a well-read student.

This punctuation is also correct:

The student was well-read.

Be sure to make a distinction between a compound modifier and the same set of words that really doesn't modify anything. It will prevent the improper use of the hyphen:

Last-minute election returns propelled her to victory.

Last-minute modifies *election returns*. Note, however:

He filed for election in the last minute of registration.

Last minute is the object of the preposition *in*. *Last* modifies only *minute*.
    Be sure to identify all parts of a compound modifier. For example, it's not a *30 mile-per-hour* speed limit. It's a *30-mile-per-hour* speed limit.

▶ **Use a hyphen for certain prefixes and suffixes.**

You'll need to consult a dictionary or stylebook in some cases. There are so many exceptions that you will never guess right all the time! For example, the Associated Press stresses this rule:

Hyphenate between the prefix and the following word if the prefix ends in a vowel and the next word begins with the same vowel (for example, *extra-attentive*; exceptions are *cooperate* and *coordinate*). Also hyphenate between the prefix and the following word if that word is capitalized (such as *super-Republican*).

Prefixes that generally take a hyphen include *all-, anti-, ex-, non-* and *pro-*. If you check a dictionary or a stylebook, however, you will find plenty of exceptions.

▶ **Use the hyphen for combinations when the preposition is omitted.**

first-come, first-served basis

a 98-94 squeaker

the push-me, pull-you dilemma

ELLIPSES

We use the *ellipsis mark* (. . .) to alert the reader that something has been removed from the original or quoted material, that the speaker has hesitated or faltered or that there is more material than is actually cited or used:

"We must fight this closure . . . we must save this factory."
(The original statement was "We must fight this closure by a management that is bent on saving money with no regard for this town; we must save this factory." In the interest of economy and impact, the writer condensed this statement but preserved its accuracy.)

Facing the hostile audience, Baker tried to frame his thoughts. "Under these circumstances," he said, "I feel I can no longer serve this community as superintendent. I have tried my best . . . I have always wanted. . . ." Unable to continue, he left the crowded meeting.

Note from this example that a period precedes the ellipsis if it ends the sentence.

▶ Other punctuation marks, if needed, come after the quoted material but before the ellipsis.

"How would you feel? . . ."

"We can't stand for this! . . ."

PARENTHESES

The characteristics of journalistic writing—brevity, crispness and clarity—imply that parentheses are not welcome but there are times when parentheses can be used effectively. Two of the most common are to signify the addition of needed information and to mark an aside to the main thought.

Caveat emptor ("let the buyer beware") should be every consumer's mantra.

He arrived at the store, only to find it was closed. (It shut down at noon for a two-hour lunch break.)

Avoid inserting lengthy or complicated material in parentheses, as a general rule.

▶ If the material inside the parentheses is not a complete sentence, put the period outside the parentheses.

She likes decaffeinated coffee (the cold-water extract type).

▶ If the parenthetical material is a complete sentence but it depends on the sentence around it for context, put the period outside the parentheses.

He whispered, "Carpe diem" ("Seize the day").

▶ If the parenthetical material is a complete sentence and can stand alone, put the period inside the parentheses.

Roads were clear this morning despite last night's heavy snowfall. (The Department of Transportation told The News this morning it had authorized overtime for three full crews.)

QUESTION MARK AND EXCLAMATION MARK

▶ **If you are asking a *direct question,* you must use the question mark.**

Why do you put peanut butter on your celery?

▶ **If your question is *indirect,* no question mark is needed.**

The nation wants to know what is happening in Iraq.

▶ **The exclamation mark should be used only to express surprise or a strong emotion.**

In most writing you probably will employ it only in direct quotation because of the exclamation's sensational nature. For example, you would not need an exclamation mark for this sentence:

The Consumer Price Index remained stable for the second consecutive month!

▶ **Both the exclamation mark and the question mark should be included inside quotation marks if the exclamation or question is part of the quoted material.**

In direct quotations, remember that the comma is not necessary if the exclamation mark or the question mark is part of the quoted material that precedes attribution:

"You can't make me answer that!" the witness screamed.

"Is this really the kind of government we want?" the senator asked.

Punctuation is more than basic mechanics. Properly used, it provides clarity, flow, emphasis—even drama. Use punctuation marks wisely and naturally to put finishing touches on your writing.

 For online activities, go to the Web site for this book at
http://communication.wadsworth.com/kessler.

CHAPTER 10

Spelling

Quickly—what's wrong with these word pairs?

definately	definitely
seperate	separate
principal	principle

Well, of the three pairs, only the last one has two correct spellings: *principal* (the head of an organization or a chief reason) and *principle* (a set of guidelines or practices that people and organizations follow). There is no such word as *definately* or *seperate*. They are misspelled, and the writer is poorer for it. We know of too many instances in which potential employers have sent an applicant's letter hurtling toward the wastebasket because it contained a spelling error.

That may seem like a harsh judgment, but that's life. At the turn of the 20th century, even famed dramatist George Bernard Shaw bemoaned the "tyranny" of spelling:

> English spelling contains thousands of excuses for rebuking children, for beating them, for imprisoning them after school hours, for breaking their spirits with impossible tasks.
> —From a letter to The Times of London

It's true—our language can be frustrating. Groups of words that have different meanings and spellings but similar sounds (such as *see/sea, meet/meat/mete, patients/patience* and *discreet/discreet*) seem to crowd our dictionaries. Then you have what seems to be an inordinate number of exceptions to spelling rules.

It's important to remember that our language is dynamic—change is always in the wind. In the area of spelling, the 200-plus-year history of our republic has seen many upheavals:

- In the wake of the American Revolution, politicians and lexicographers joined forces to create some "American" spellings (*theater, honor,*

119

defense) so they wouldn't be the same as the British spellings *(theatre, honour, defence).*

- A U.S. president, a notoriously poor speller, unsuccessfully tried to strong-arm the U.S. Congress to adopt some spelling changes.

- A newspaper publisher—who didn't need Congress to adopt new spellings—created his own *(altho, fantom, thru)* and mandated that his paper use them. (It did, until some years after his death.)

Then there was the creation of the Simplified Spelling Society, which ironically required a 42-word alphabet.

Let's face it: Neither computer spell-checkers nor a desperate hope that a kindly editor will bail you out will avoid the inevitable. To be a good speller, you must recognize and understand a great number of words, and you must *see* them properly. Let's first talk about recognizing improper spellings, then we'll suggest a regimen to help you improve your spelling. First, we look at seeing and hearing, then at a careful review of work to combat misspellings.

RECOGNIZING MISSPELLINGS: WHAT'S IN YOUR MEMORY BANK?

It doesn't necessarily follow that serious readers are good spellers, but a steady diet of the printed word can't hurt. In an electronic age in which we hear far more words than we see, we have fewer opportunities to visualize words and to understand their meanings. When we don't *see* these words, our retention of them and their context suffers. For example, it helps to see the word *environment* because the *n* in *environ* (its root) is often not properly pronounced.

The same is true for two similar-sounding adjectives: *discreet* (prudent or cautious) and *discrete* (distinct or separate). Seeing these words in the context of their proper use greatly helps the imprinting process:

The diplomats arranged for a <u>discreet</u> meeting.

Your instructions have three <u>discrete</u> parts.

Hearing these words can also give us some context for their use, but complete visualization is key to completing our understanding and future proper use.

Making the correct choice between *stationary* (not moving) and *stationery* (writing material) may not seem difficult, as the two words are quite different in meaning. Yet how often are they confused and therefore misspelled? Then there's the matter of *sweet* versus *suite*, or *desert* versus *dessert*, and *complimentary* versus *complementary*. As you can tell, this could become a very long list! Our advice: See the word. Note the organization of its letters. Link that to its meaning and use. When you do that, you won't get confused over the spelling and word use in this sentence:

The $40-a-day <u>suite</u> was a <u>sweet</u> deal, especially with its <u>complimentary</u> <u>dessert</u>.

Learning to Listen

Note the sounds of these two words:

Pronounce: Pro-nouns′

Pronunciation: Pro-nun-see-á-shun

By listening to yourself say these words, can you *see* the difference in their spellings? Note, for example, the "ow" in *pronounce* and the "un" in *pronunciation,* and it's likely that you won't mistakenly spell out *pronounciation.* Again, seeing these words helps our imprinting.

Now consider these two words: *wreck,* as a verb (pronounced "rek" with a soft *e,* meaning to destroy accidentally) and *wreak* (pronounced "reek" and meaning to inflict punishment or damage). Not understanding the proper pronunciation of a word and its meaning led to this erroneous (and embarrassing) newspaper headline:

Storm <u>Wrecks</u> Havoc on Fishing Village

Fortunately, the study of *phonics* (teaching reading and spelling with the sounds of speech) is enjoying a resurgence, after some bitter wars over such controversial curricula as "whole language." There is even a best-selling computer program available for children, widely advertised on television. This should reinforce the contention that although some language can be acquired by intuition and guesswork, serious understandings of what words mean, how they are used, how they are arranged in sentences and exactly how they are spelled are all directly related to in-depth instruction in phonics, reading and meaning.

Proofreading: The Perceptive Review

In our experience many weak spellers are not careful readers of their own work. They are "skimmers," who glide distractedly over what they have written, not carefully examining either structure or content, in the belief that their work is done. Therefore, they won't be alert to checking words that appear suspicious. They may not assume that a certain percentage of the words they use may be spelled incorrectly. And, worst of all, they don't (or won't) look up the word to check meaning and spelling.

Proofreading is a vital part of editing. This process requires close attention to one's writing—its content, meaning, structure and spelling. Although a spell-checker can be effective as an alert system, we say: Live with your dictionary. Inhale it. Understand the look, meaning and sound of words. And read, read and read some more. You will be amazed at how your word recognition will improve.

KEYS TO IMPROVING YOUR SPELLING

We believe that there are three keys to spelling improvement: sound, sense and structure. They provide an effective approach, which brings you closer to your language.

Sound

"Sounding out" a word by breaking it into phonetic patterns can be an effective spelling guide. It's amazing how many words you can sound out without the aid of a dictionary and come up with the right spelling. English is a tricky language, however, full of oddities that can slip you up. Look at the following words, which all have the same -*ough* ending:

through   cough   bough   dough
(throo)   (kôf)   (bow, sounding like "ow") (doe—with a long *o*)

Similar spellings, four different sounds—it's another one of the challenges of English spelling. Looking up a word also reveals how many syllables it has and which syllable is accented. This provides a fine tuning of the word.

Consider these two nouns:

desert—barren wilderness
(déz-urt)

dessert—something sweet after a meal
(di-zúrt)

Their differing pronunciations should help distinguish their difference in spellings. Naturally, exceptions always spoil the example, so in the interest of full disclosure we admit that the verb *desert* (to abandon) is pronounced like the noun *dessert*. (Nothing's perfect, right?) Examining syllables will also give you a keener ear for pronunciation.

A method sometimes used to help improve spelling is mnemonics (beginning *m* is silent), which means a device to help one's memory or, in the case of spelling, to create a memorable association. In the case of *dessert*, we suggest a sweet treat that is so good that you want *two* helpings—leading you to remember the two *s*'s in the word.

Here are two often-misspelled words, broken into their syllables. Note how a careful sounding of them helps you avoid a misspelling:

di-lem-ma
(not two 's and one *m*)

sep-a-rate
(*sep* and *rate* are not separated by an *e*. Further, the *a* is sounded as an "ah," not "urh," which, as your dictionary explains, indicates an *e*.)

Checking pronunciation also makes you aware of silent (but not invisible) letters that can foil your spelling. For example, the musical *chord* has a silent *h*, which makes it sound exactly like the material *cord*. The normal pronunciation of *government* does not reveal the hidden *n*, yet in this case *govern* is an obvious root. The same goes for a hidden *r* in *surprise*, although there is no sensible root here that will assist you.

Sound may be a great help in unraveling and then putting together difficult words, but making sense of meaning also plays a key role.

Sense

What does this word mean? What is its proper use in a sentence? Answering these questions often requires the use of a dictionary, or some closer examination of the history and use of a word. A dividend of such a search is that you will see the correct spelling of the word. When you see certain word pairs together, perhaps you immediately understand the differences in their meanings—and spellings. But you would rarely see them together, so it helps to set up pairs (even trios) and study them with an eye toward their spelling differences.

Look at the following *homophones* (similar-sounding word pairs). You probably can define the differences between many of them, but how quickly can you adjust to their different spellings? That part of seeing—and understanding—a word, especially in the context of a sentence, is critical to its proper use and spelling. It reflects not just on your general knowledge but on your precision as well. As you will note, your mastery of the parts of speech will be important in recognizing the distinctions among these groups.

accept	crews	morning	rack	to
except	cruise	mourning	wrack	too
aisle	discreet	oar	rye	two
isle	discrete	ore	wry	vain
bear	grate	penance	seam	vane
bare	great	pennants	seem	vein
berry	heard	pray	sight	ware
bury	herd	prey	site	wear
cede	hour	principal	cite	where
seed	our	principle	their	weather
complement	lead	profit	there	whether
compliment	led	prophet	they're	

Understanding the sense of a word helps us to both use and spell it correctly. Consider *council* and *counsel*. Similar pronunciations aside, their intended meanings in the sentence should be clear:

The city <u>council</u> adjourned without a decision, based on advice from its legal <u>counsel</u>.

The attorney <u>counseled</u> his client to appeal the zoning decision to the city <u>council</u>.

These distinctions are cheerfully brought to you by your dictionary.

The subject–verb contraction *it's* and the possessive pronoun *its* are other examples in which spelling depends on knowing the sense of words. In this case good grammar requires us to know the difference between *it's* and *its*, but a knowledge of their meanings is a giant step toward avoiding errors in their selection. It's not that difficult, right?

Structure

Just as our language has rules dealing with agreement, case and punctuation, it has rules to control spelling as well. It may seem as though spelling rules are riddled with exceptions, but most words are covered by some basic guidelines. Let's examine several of the key rules—and deal gingerly with the exceptions.

Surviving suffixes

A *suffix* is a group of letters added to the end of a root word to give it new or added meaning. For example, when you add *ible* to *access*, you have *accessible*, which means "easy to approach."

Sometimes, however, suffixes are tacked on to incomplete roots. Take *dispense*. If you want a suffix after it to denote "an ability to dispense," you would add *able*, and because the last letter of the root is a vowel, you drop it and make *dispensable*. (As you might expect, dropping the vowel doesn't always occur.)

Why, you might ask, do we have *-ible* and *-able* when they mean the same thing? The answer has to do with the history of our language; *-ible* connects with Old Latin–based verbs, and *-able* has Old French and Anglo-Saxon lineage. The use of *-able* or *-ible* gives you a clue to a word's origin, and you will find that *-able* words outnumber the *-ible* ones.

The other suffixes you should master are *-ance/-ence* and *-ant/-ent*. These too come from French and Latin, and the *-a* or *-e* choice has to do only with the original form of the Latin or French word.

Both *-ance* and *-ence* create nouns from verbs, indicating a state or a quality, as in *resistance* and *persistence*. Both *-ant* and *-ent* are used to form adjectives, as in *resistant* and *persistent*.

Given this background, we can offer the following general rules about the uses of these suffixes.

▶ **Not only is -able more common than -ible but it also is used mostly with complete root words.**

Therefore, we have *workable, dependable* and *perishable*. There are, of course, exceptions. A few root words drop their final *e* when adding *-able*. These include *desirable, excusable, indispensable* and *usable*. Fortunately, there aren't many of these! There are many more examples of the retention of the final *e*, such as *changeable, manageable* and *noticeable*.

▶ **Only -able follows g, i and the hard c ("k" sound).**

This dependable rule explains the spelling of *navigable, amiable* and *irrevocable*. It does require an understanding of the usable "root" form, however, as in *navig* for *navigate*.

▶ **The suffix -ible is commonly used after double consonants (such as ll), and after s, st, some "d" sounds and the soft c ("s" sound).**

This rule explains *infallible* and *horrible, divisible* and *plausible, edible* and *credible, forcible* and *invincible.*

▶ **Sorry to say, but there are no firm rules for the use of -*ance*/-*ence* and -*ant*/-*ent* suffixes.**

There are some guidelines, however, to help you make some distinctions:

- Their sounds. For example, *attendance* has an "ah" sound in its suffix, but *independence* has an "eh" sound.

- Your memory. Here are some of the more difficult ones to remember:

-ance/-ant	-ence/-ent
attendance	existence
descendant	independence
maintenance	persistent
relevant	recurrent
resistant	superintendent

Ie-Ei-Oh!

The *ie/ei* dilemma is not overwhelming. The following guidelines should help.

▶ **The -*ie* spelling is more common than -*ei*. And *i* usually precedes *e* unless it follows a *c* that carries an "s" sound.**

Here are some examples:

Before or without a *c*	After a *c*
fierce	deceit
hygiene	perceive
niece	receipt
wield	receive

Note that French -*ier* words like *financier* don't violate the -*ei* after *c* rule. The -*ier* just happens to be a standard ending.

It's more demanding to master those -*ei* constructions:

- Words with long "a" sounds, such as *weigh* and *freight*

- Words with long "an" sounds, such as *feign* and *reign*

- Five exceptions that just demand memorization: *caffeine, leisure, protein, seize* and *weird*

▶ **If a *c* carries a "sh" sound, it probably will be followed by *ie*.**

Examples include:

ancient deficient sufficient

To double or not to double the consonant

When you add *ing* or *ed* to a word, you generally double a final consonant only when:

- The word ends in a single consonant: *Commit* becomes *committing* and *committed*.

- That consonant is preceded by a single vowel: *Commit* is safe here, so the final consonant can be doubled.

- The accent is on the last syllable: The pronunciation is *com<u>mit</u>* (accented syllable underlined), so our rule is valid.

Note these other examples, where all three guidelines are met:

acquitted equipping occurring omitted

Once you understand this rule, you can see that certain words will not double their final consonant. This occurs when:

- The accent is not on the final syllable of the root word. This explains *canceled* and *traveling*. Note their accents:

<u>can</u>cel <u>tra</u>vel

This also explains the spelling of *profited*.

- No vowel precedes the final consonant. This explains *investing;* a consonant precedes the final *t*.

Take note of one other guideline: The suffix *-ment* doesn't require doubling the final consonant of the root word. Because *-ment* begins with a consonant, there is no need to alter the root:

equipping *but* equipment

allotting *but* allotment

committed *but* commitment

That battalion of harassing and embarrassing words

Explanation almost fails when we discuss the next list of words, which are frustrating but not overwhelming. Although reliable rules seem to have been abandoned, sound can be a great help. Examining differences in pronunciations and meanings can help, too.

This list of troublesome word groups is not comprehensive, but it should help you in many cases:

accumulate	inoculate	recommend
accommodate	innovative	occasional
battalion	millionaire	religious
medallion	questionnaire	sacrilegious
census	proceed	theater
consensus	precede	massacre
embarrass	supersede	vilify
harass		villain

SOME FINAL WORDS (TO REMEMBER!)

Here is a list of difficult spellings that vex many writers—some of the words most commonly misspelled by students and professionals. Note that many of the guidelines and suggestions mentioned in this chapter can help you spell these words correctly.

Remember: *When in doubt, look it up.*

acceptable	bookkeeper	desirable	indispensable
accessible	broccoli	desperate	innocuous
accidentally	business	deterrent	inoculate
accommodate	caffeine	dilemma	irascible
accumulate	calendar	ecstasy	irresistible
acknowledgment	canceled	eighth	jeopardy
acquit	cemetery	embarrass	judgment
adviser	changeable	environment	legitimate
a lot	commitment	excusable	leisure
all ready	comparable	exhilarate	likable
already	condemn	existence	likelihood
annihilate	conscious	financier	loneliness
argument	consensus	forcible	manageable
athletic	courageous	harassment	millionaire
bankruptcy	criticize	hemorrhage	misspell
believe	definite	hygiene	niece

noticeable	predecessor	seizure	vacillate
occasion	privilege	separate	vacuum
occurrence	procedure	sheriff	vilify
omitted	protein	skillful	villian
optimistic	questionnaire	sovereign	weird
parallel	recommend	succeed	wield
permissible	relevant	supersede	willful
persistent	repetitious	surprise	withhold
potatoes	resistant	tariff	woolly
precede	rhythm	temperament	yield

For online activities, go to the Web site for this book at
http://communication.wadsworth.com/kessler.

CHAPTER 11

Clarity, Conciseness, Coherence

If you think clear, crisp writing flows effortlessly from the pens of good writers, you're wrong. Good writing is hard, purposeful work. Veteran writers care about each choice of word, the creation of each clause, sentence and paragraph. They know that direct, powerful writing says *precisely* what the author means to say—no more, no less, no ambiguity, no blurry meanings, no wasted words, no flabby prose. They know that this kind of writing is the result of many decisions mindfully made, many questions thoughtfully asked. *What am I trying to say? Is this what I mean? Is it precisely what I mean? Is this the very best way to say what I mean?*

Writers who care about the quality of their work constantly question themselves as they write, edit and revise. Then, word by word, sentence by sentence, paragraph by paragraph, they create clear, forceful prose. You can, too.

CHOOSING WORDS

As we form ideas about what we want to say, we are immediately confronted with the most fundamental choice: the individual word. The words we choose must communicate precisely what we mean with a minimum of fuss and a maximum of power. This is particularly true with verbs, the engines of the sentence. Choosing the *correct* verb is a matter of grammar; choosing the *right* verb is a matter of conciseness and clarity. Consider the following word choice problems, remembering that every choice, no matter how minor, no matter how seemingly mechanical, affects the clarity of your prose.

Avoiding *Up*

She was chosen to <u>head up</u> the investigation.

The president must <u>face up</u> to the issues.

The construction <u>slowed up</u> [down] traffic all morning.

None of these verbs needs the preposition *up*. All of them are weakened by the extra word. *Up* doesn't add meaning to these verbs; it takes away crispness. This may seem like a minor point, but it is at this basic level that good writing begins.

She was chosen to <u>head</u> the investigation.

The president must <u>face</u> the issues.

The construction <u>slowed</u> traffic all morning.

Beware of *free up* (free), *wake up* (awake), *stand up* (stand) and *shake up* (shake). In these instances *up* is more than unnecessary; it is sloppy.

Of course some verbs need *up* to complete their meaning. *Make* does not mean the same thing as *make up*. *Break* is not synonymous with *break up*. *Up* is necessary for the meaning of *pick up*. In these cases *up* is not clutter, but neither is it strong, precise writing.

He accused the senator of <u>making up</u> the allegations.
(weak)
He accused the senator of <u>fabricating</u> the allegations.
(stronger)

The investigation <u>broke up</u> the crime syndicate.
(weak)
The investigation <u>shattered</u> the crime syndicate.
(stronger)

The economy is <u>picking up</u>.
(weak)
The economy is <u>recovering</u>.
(stronger)

"Verbizing" Nouns

The committee must <u>prioritize</u> its concerns, <u>concretize</u> its goals, <u>definitize</u> its objectives and <u>operationalize</u> its plan before it <u>fractionalizes</u> the community and <u>destabilizes</u> its natural constituency.

The suffix -*ize* is on the loose, "verbizing" and "uglyizing" our language. Some people think you can tack *ize* onto any noun and create a verb. Most of those makeshift verbs are unnecessary. *Fractionalize*, for example, means nothing more than *split*. Other words with longer linguistic histories, such as *utilize* and *signalize*, serve no distinct purpose. *Utilize* has come to mean nothing more than *use*. *Signalize* means signal. Not only are many of these -*ize* words useless but they are also grating to the ear and uncomfortably bureaucratic.

Of course, yesterday's awkward jargon is today's respectable word. *Pasteurize* must have raised the hackles of 19th-century grammarians, but few would be upset about it today. It is difficult to say how many of the newly created, tongue-twisting -*ize* verbs will become permanent additions to our language. (They fewer the better, we hope.) While we are all awaiting the verdict, we can subject an awkward-sounding -*ize* verb to three tests:

1. Is it listed in the dictionary as an acceptable (not informal, colloquial or slang) word?

2. Does it have a unique meaning?

3. Does it have a sound that is, at the very least, not displeasing?

If the word passes the three tests, use it. If it fails, find another word. Do not "jargonize" and "awkwardize" the language. It may be all right to *pasteurize* milk, but it is not yet acceptable to *chocolatize* it.

That

That performs several grammatical functions. It is an adjective:

That book changed my life.
(*That* describes book.)

It is a demonstrative pronoun:

That will change your life.
(*That* takes the place of a noun.)

It is a relative pronoun:

This is a book that will change your life.
(*That* introduces a relative clause.)

It is a conjunction:

The author said that writing the book changed her life.
(*That* links two independent clauses.)

The troublesome uses of *that* are as a conjunction and as a relative pronoun. Simply put, writers overuse the word. *That* is often unnecessary in a sentence. Its inclusion often robs the sentence of its grace and rhythm. If a word does not add meaning, get rid of it. Consider these sentences, all of which would be crisper without *that:*

The author said t~~hat~~ writing the book changed her life.

The researchers admitted t~~hat~~ they falsified data.

Government sources say t~~hat~~ the study is flawed.

Often all you need do is remove the useless *that;* however, some sentences demand revision. Conciseness is the issue:

This is a book that will change your life.
(wordy)
This book will change your life.
(improved)

Police recovered the limousine that was stolen.
(wordy)
Police recovered the stolen limousine.
(improved)

The photograph that she took won first prize.
(wordy)
Her photograph won first prize.
(improved)

That is sometimes used legitimately to link sentence parts. To discover whether *that* is necessary to a sentence, ask yourself two questions:

1. Can *that* be eliminated with no change in the meaning of the sentence?

2. Can the clause introduced by *that* be expressed more succinctly?

If you answer *yes* to either question, edit or rewrite.

Redundancy and Wordiness

In the world of writing, less is often more: the economical phrase, the lean sentence, the stark image. They grab the reader. They remain in the reader's mind. On the other hand, clutter—words that serve no purpose—interfere with clear and memorable communication.

Make your words count. Ignorance of the real meanings of words, attempts at false erudition, repetition of other people's jargon, murky thinking and sheer sloppiness can all result in prose that is wordy or redundant. Consider these examples of redundancy:

mutual cooperation
(*Cooperation* means "acting for mutual benefit." *Mutual* is redundant.)

end result
(*Result,* by definition, is the consequence.)

very unique
(*Unique* is one of a kind. It either is or isn't.)

incumbent officeholder
(The definition of *incumbent* is "officeholder.")

consensus of opinion
(*Consensus* means "collective opinion.")

repeat again
(*Repeat* includes "again" in its definition.)

refer back
(*Refer* includes "back" in its definition.)

more universal
more universally accepted
(*Universal* means "worldwide." How can it be more than worldwide?)

A number of wordy, sluggish expressions have crept into writing. Here are some of the more common ones to avoid:

Instead of	Use
as of now	now
at the present time	now
at this point in time	now
despite the fact that	although
due to the fact that	because
on account of	because
seeing as how	because
during the course of	during

Vague Words

When we speak, thinking as we talk, sometimes searching for words or fumbling with thoughts, we often insert such meaningless vagaries as *a type of, a kind of,* or *in terms of.* You might hear yourself say something like this one day: "It was the type of thing I was kind of proud of, I mean in terms of personal accomplishments." That's bad enough in speech. It is absolutely inadmissible in writing. The solution: Think before you write, then edit, edit, edit.

Years of writing term papers and hearing dense and sluggish bureaucratic language—some of it, unfortunately, passed along by journalists—have cemented in our minds such filler words as *aspect, element, factor, situation, character,* and *condition.*

The aspect of the situation that will be a factor will depend on the character of the elements we must contend with.

This is what you say—or write—when you don't know what you're talking about. The result is not only the opposite of clear writing; it is the opposite of *any* communication. Should these words crop up in your prose, weed them out mercilessly.

Euphemisms and "Fancy Words"

When people or organizations want to protect themselves or hide bad news or take the edge off potentially offensive information, they create *euphemisms*—generally vague, often purposefully misleading, but inoffensive ways of saying (or not saying) what they mean. When the Internal Revenue Service finally stopped pursuing a taxpayer who had, in fact, done nothing wrong, the agency sent this note:

The audit issue was reconsidered and determined not to have existed.

Audit issue is sanitized code for a fierce, three-year battle between the taxpayer and the agency. *Reconsidered,* in this case, means the IRS finally figured out it was wrong. Note how skillfully this eerie sentence substitutes clear expression—*we made a mistake*—with euphemism. The sentence is carefully constructed to obscure an admission of error.

Euphemisms are all around us. A company, deeply in debt, might announce to its stockholders that it is "currently experiencing a budgetary shortfall." Another, found guilty of dumping toxic waste in a river, might admit that its "environmental compliance statistics showed a downturn." The military wins the dubious prize for creating both the most and the most chilling euphemisms. *Entry into a nonpermissive environment* is the military's way of evading the word *invasion. Friendly fire* softens the terrible tragedy of the action it describes: gunfire against troops by their own troops. *Collateral damage* is a euphemism for killing civilians.

Let's say it's snowing outside with a wind chill factor of 10 below zero, and you look out the window and see a man running down the street clad only in boxers. What would you most likely say? What would clearly, precisely and directly express the moment? "Look at that guy! He must be nuts!" A master of euphemism would see the same thing and quietly comment that the man was "somewhat inappropriately attired given the climatic conditions." Writers can't stop others from manufacturing euphemisms, but they can refuse to transmit them.

A related clarity problem is "fancy words." We don't mean three-dollar words like *prestidigitation* or *ovolactovegetarianism*. We mean silly, inflated words that take the place of good, plain, ordinary, serviceable words: *facility* for building, *infrastructure* for roads and bridges, *domicile* for home. Stay clear of these pretensions. If others use them, your responsibility as a public communicator is to *not* pass them on.

Jargon

The first meaning of the word *jargon*, one dictionary tells us, is "meaningless chatter." Of course, the word is more commonly understood to mean the specialized language of a trade or a profession. But as writers we ought to take to heart that first definition. To our audience, jargon is, more often than not, meaningless chatter.

Scientific, technical and scholarly diction insulates members of a profession from the outside world, excluding "nonmembers" from what is being said. "Members" may talk or write to one another in jargon, using it as shorthand or code. That's one thing. But *public* communicators—media writers—have a responsibility to communicate clearly and simply to wider audiences. Writers should be jargon slayers not jargon purveyors.

Here is a scientist deep in the throes of jargon:

Despite rigid reexamination of all experimental variables, this protocol continued to produce data at variance with our subsequently proven hypothesis.
(*Translation:* The experiment didn't work.)

Here is cop talk:

While doing OPs to watch a set, we raised the player and he beelined.
(*Translation:* During observation of a drug deal, the dealer got wind of the cops and fled.)

Jargon can be used to obscure ideas or make ordinary ideas sound more important. It can also be used to hide meaning or desensitize people to issues. For a writer to perpetuate such jargon signals a profound failure to communicate.

Although jargon may serve a purpose for those within a profession, it serves no purpose in public writing. Using jargon does not make you sound impressive. On the contrary, you impress (and help) your audience by lucidly explaining difficult material, not repeating words and phrases you do not understand.

PUTTING WORDS TOGETHER

Clear, concise, coherent writing depends on more than careful word choice. Proper placement of words is imperative. Misplacement mistakes can easily harm the clarity of your prose.

Misplaced Words

In a sentence, a modifier needs to point directly and clearly to what it modifies. This generally means placing the modifier next to or as close as possible to what it is modifying. Adverbs like *only, nearly, almost, just, scarcely, even, hardly* and *merely* create the biggest potential difficulty because their placement can drastically change the meaning of the sentence. Note how placement changes meaning in the following examples:

Only he can help you.
(No one else can help you.)

He can only help you.
(He can't do anything more than help you.)

He can help only you.
(He can't help anyone else.)

Notice how the placement of *almost* in the next two sentences changes the meaning:

Negotiations almost broke down on every clause in the contract.
(Negotiations did not quite break down.)

Negotiations broke down on almost every clause in the contract.
(Just about every clause caused problems during negotiations.)

When we speak we often have a devil-may-care attitude toward the placement of adverbs. But, because placement most surely and definitely changes meaning, stick to the old rule: Place the adverb (or other word) next to or as close as possible to the word you intend it to modify.

Misplaced Phrases and Clauses

Like individual words, phrases and clauses should be placed next to or near what they modify. Again, placement affects meaning, as these examples illustrate:

Dozens of homes were devastated by wildfires <u>across the Southwest</u>.

Dozens of homes <u>across the Southwest</u> were devastated by wildfires.

Note how the phrase *across the Southwest* in the first sentence modifies *wildfires*. The meaning here is that the entire Southwest region experienced wildfires. In the second sentence, we do not know how large an area was affected by the fires. Perhaps there was a series of small, local fires. We do know that Southwestern homes were devastated.

The plan <u>that the student council is debating</u> will alter the university's free speech policy.

The plan will alter the university's free speech policy <u>that the student council is debating</u>.

In the first sentence, the *plan* is being debated. In the second example, the *policy* is being debated.

Dangling Modifiers

A modifier "dangles" when what it is supposed to modify is not part of the sentence. For example:

To be successful in this business, perseverance is needed.

The phrase *to be successful in this business* does not modify anything in the sentence. The only word it could modify is *perseverance*, but that makes no sense. The sentence needs to be revised:

To be successful in this business, you must persevere.

Now the phrase correctly modifies *you*. Not only that, the revised sentence is in the active voice. The dangling-modifier sentence was in the passive voice. Here is another dangling modifier:

After studying for more than three years, Spanish came easily to him.

Clearly, *Spanish* did not do the studying; *he* did. Coherence is at stake here. The sentence needs to be rewritten so the introductory phrase clearly modifies the correct word:

After studying for more than three years, he found Spanish easy to master.

Split Constructions

Just as modifiers need to rest closely to what they modify, so other parts of the sentence must be placed carefully to maintain clarity and coherence of thought.

Split verbs often lead to incoherence. In most cases it is best to keep auxiliary verbs next to the main verb and to avoid splitting infinitives. Consider what happens to sentence unity and graceful expression when you separate auxiliary verbs from the main verb:

Refugees <u>have been</u> for more than three months <u>living</u> in temporary camps near the border.
(auxiliary and main verb split)

For more than three months, refugees <u>have been living</u> in temporary camps near the border.
(improved)

The more words you place between the verb parts, the less coherent the sentence becomes. Occasionally, however, it is acceptable—even preferable—to split a multipart verb. Almost always the verb is split by a single word, an adverb:

Noise <u>has</u> always <u>been</u> a problem in the apartment complex.

Placing *always* between the verb parts does not hinder coherence. In fact, it adds emphasis.

Infinitives (*to* forms of the verb) should also, in most cases, remain intact. Split infinitives contribute to awkwardness and interfere with coherent expression. A sentence should read smoothly and make sense:

Police officials promised <u>to</u> as soon as possible <u>look</u> into the noise problem.
(split infinitive)

Police officials promised <u>to look</u> into the noise problem as soon as possible.
(improved)

To aid sentence clarity and help readers or listeners understand quickly what you are trying to say, keep the subject and the verb as close as possible. Look what happens to coherence when subject and verb are interrupted by lengthy explanatory material:

The <u>agency</u>, following weeks of internal debate that resulted in the
   (subj.)
reshuffling of hundreds of employees, <u>restructured</u> two of its bureaus.
                                                    (verb)

The sentence forces readers or listeners to wade through 14 words between the subject *(agency)* and its verb *(restructured)*. But readers may have neither the time nor the inclination to slog through such constructions, and listeners can easily lose the thread of meaning. Be kind to your audience. Keep subject and verb close:

> The <u>agency</u> <u>restructured</u> two of its bureaus following weeks of internal
>   (subj.) (verb)
> debate that resulted in the reshuffling of hundreds of employees.

Consider one more common splitting problem: a verb and its complements. The simplest construction to understand is subject-verb-object. It answers the basic question *Who did what to whom?* Just as splitting the subject *(who)* from the verb *(did what)* interferes with clarity and coherence, so too does splitting the verb *(did what)* from its complement *(to whom)*. Keep the verb and its complements (object, adverb, descriptive phrase) as close together as possible. You will promote sentence unity, readability and coherence. Consider this example:

> Consumer advocates <u>protested</u> yesterday morning in front of three
>   (verb)
> local toy stores <u>what they say is the marketing of violence to children</u>
>   (complement)
> <u>through the sale of toy guns.</u>

This sentence is clumsy. To avoid losing coherent thought—and your audience—rewrite:

> Consumer advocates protested today what they say is the marketing of violence to children through the sale of toy guns. Marching [picketing, assembling, gathering] in front of three local toy stores, they . . .

MAKING SENSE

Every good grammatical decision you make contributes to clarity, conciseness and coherence. Choosing strong, precise words is the first step. Placing these words correctly is the next. Focusing on the architecture of sentences is the third level.

Parallel Structure

When you place like ideas in like grammatical patterns, you create *parallel structure.* As we discussed in Chapter 6, parallel structure aligns related ideas and presents them through the repetition of grammatical structure. It is vital to both clarity and unity, and helps create rhythm and grace in a sentence. To create parallel structure using single words, you use a series of words that are the same part of speech. For example:

This recent erosion of our civil liberties is <u>unwarranted</u>, <u>unfair</u> and <u>indefensible</u>.

The related ideas are the criticisms of the erosion of civil liberties. The grammatical pattern is the repetition of single adjectives.

To create parallel structure using phrases or clauses, replicate the grammatical pattern:

Meditating can <u>clear your mind</u>, <u>relax your body</u> and <u>lift your spirits</u>.
(repeating phrases)

Because we have the resources, because we know what's right and because we have no other choice, we should rid our air and water of toxic chemicals.
(repeating clauses)

Parallel structure binds ideas and enhances the audience's understanding of each idea by creating a lucid pattern. If you begin a sentence by establishing a particular grammatical pattern and then break the implicit contract you have made with your audience, you create confusion and disharmony.

Parallel structure is commonly used to introduce complementary, contrasting or sequential ideas. The relationship between the ideas can be implicit (as in the examples offered thus far) or it can be made apparent by using signal words:

- Complementary relationship: *both/and, not only/but also*

- Contrasting relationship: *either/or, neither/nor*

- Sequential relationship: *first/second/third*

<u>Both</u> the construction of bike lanes <u>and</u> the rerouting of delivery trucks should ease traffic in the university district.
(complementary relationship, parallel structure)

<u>Either</u> we enforce the clean air standards <u>or</u> we all buy gas masks.
(contrasting relationship, parallel structure)

<u>First</u>, define the problem; <u>second</u>, gather the information; <u>third</u>, brainstorm the alternatives.
(sequential relationship, parallel structure)

Whether you make the relationship explicit by using signal words or implicit by letting the ideas speak for themselves, parallel structure is vital to clarity and coherence.

Sentence Fragments

As you remember from Chapter 5, a *fragment* is a group of words that lacks a subject, a predicate, a complete thought or any combination of the three. Grammatically, a fragment cannot stand alone. When readers see a group of words beginning with a capital letter and ending with a period, they expect a complete sentence. If instead you offer them a fragment, you confuse them. Unintentional fragments hinder both coherence and clarity.

> Amazon.com has revolutionized the art of bookselling. Although the online service has its drawbacks.

This fragment (underlined) hinders meaning and clarity. Perhaps the writer meant:

> Although the online service has its drawbacks, Amazon.com has revolutionized the art of bookselling.

Maybe the writer meant no such connection. Perhaps the fragment was meant to signal the beginning of a new idea:

> Amazon.com has revolutionized the art of bookselling. Although the online service has its drawbacks, millions of buyers find it fast and convenient.

Fragments leave your audience hanging, forcing them to guess your intended meaning. Offer clear, complete thoughts. Fragments used knowingly, sparingly and stylistically are another story. See Chapter 12 for a more in-depth discussion.

Run-On Sentences

A *run-on sentence* is composed of two, three or any number of whole, complete sentences joined together ungrammatically. Chapter 5 discussed the run-on as a grammatical problem. Here we want to emphasize it as an obstacle to concise and coherent writing.

The two most common run-on sentences are those inappropriately linked with *and* and those incorrectly spliced with commas. Both can confuse and frustrate a reader:

The university must deal with a shrinking budget and class sizes will increase.
(run-on)

When you use *and* to link two independent clauses as above, you are saying that the two thoughts reinforce or directly complement each other or follow one another sequentially. If this isn't the case, as in the preceding example, you have created not just a run-on but also an incoherent sentence. If the thoughts in the clauses are not related in a definable, explicit way, rewrite the run-on as two separate sentences. If the thoughts are related, use a connecting word to signal the correct relationship:

Because the university must deal with a shrinking budget, class sizes will increase.
(improved)

Note that the run-on was corrected by subordinating one thought (clause) to another to clarify and make explicit the relationship between the two clauses.

When commas link clauses, readers expect the words following a comma to add to or complement what they have just read. If the clauses are not related in this way, the result is an incoherent run-on:

The legislature mandated cutbacks throughout the university, class sizes increased dramatically, class offerings decreased significantly.

This run-on sentence needs to be rewritten with the relationship between the clauses clearly expressed. Commas are the wrong signal here. In the absence of correct signals, it is unclear exactly what relationship exists. Here's a rewrite:

Soon after the legislature mandated cutbacks throughout the university, class size increased dramatically, and class offerings decreased significantly.

Now the relationship between the three thoughts is clear.

CLARITY, CONCISENESS, COHERENCE

Writers write to be understood. Whether they are writing to inform, amuse, uplift, persuade or cajole, their thoughts must be clear; their sentences must be comprehensible. Clarity, conciseness and coherence begin with individual word choice. From that point every grammatical decision either enhances or detracts from this triple goal. Imprecision, clutter, misplaced phrases and murky construction have no place in good writing. The goal is lean, powerful communication. It is not an easy goal. But with practice, patience, hard work and a firm grasp of grammar, it is an attainable one.

For online activities, go to the Web site for this book at
http://communication.wadsworth.com/kessler.

CHAPTER 12

Style

What could possibly compel you to read—and actually enjoy—a story about Tupperware or an essay on the liver or an article on the origin of the pencil? It's not much of a challenge to write a story others will read when the subject you're tackling is inherently dramatic—miners trapped 300 feet below the surface—or has immediate relevance to their lives, like an approaching hurricane. But what about the stories people read or attend to not because they were already interested but because the writer *made* them interested?

How does a writer do that? How does a writer make a piece on Tupperware a must-read? The key is learning to go beyond correctness, clarity and competence to something more: to stylish, graceful, compelling writing. This is not an easy task. It is, after all, a writer's life work, the evolution of craft. Style doesn't just happen. It is carefully, thoughtfully, imaginatively and patiently built.

WHAT IS STYLE?

Style is the writer's unique vision—and the lively, original expression of that vision—that draws audience attention to the message. It is the reflection of the writer's individual way of seeing, thinking and using language. It is the product of purposeful choices, the culmination of many small things done well, the result of sheer hard work. Style has an important place in *all* writing.

Novice writers, and many experienced ones as well, harbor several dangerous misconceptions about style:

- They believe if they write clean, clutterless prose, their writing will lack style.

- They believe style is like a garnish or a spicy condiment added to bring zip to bland writing. They believe style has something to do with ornamentation or flashiness.

- They fear that style, because it is hard to define ("I don't know what it is, but I know it when I see it"), is therefore mysterious and unattainable.

They are wrong.

As any sophisticated writer will tell you, style emerges from—and cannot exist without—crisp, lean, language use. First come the fundamentals: strong verbs, grammatical consistency, tightly constructed sentences. Then comes style. Novelist John Updike looks at style by comparing the process of writing to the process of becoming a musician. Musicians begin by learning to identify and play individual notes. They learn how to read music. They practice scales. They play simple compositions. Only after mastering these fundamentals can they begin to develop their own manner of musical expression, their own style. Writers too must master the basics before they can find their own voice.

Style, then, has little to do with ostentatious language. Window dressing (a gaggle of adjectives, for example), verbal ornamentation (big words or purple prose) and fancy tricks do not generally contribute to compelling writing. In fact, verbal flashiness can obscure coherent thought. There is nothing flashy, but everything compelling, about these first two paragraphs of a Wall Street Journal story written by Carrie Dolan:

> Out on an open range, a 1,300-pound bull with ropes looped around his middle stands drooling in the dust. He is stubbornly resisting efforts to load him into a stock trailer so he can be taken to the corral for medical treatment.
>
> Jane Glennie gets out of her truck. She spits into her hand and grinds a glowing cigarette butt into her palm. While two mounted cowboys hold the ropes tight, she plants her boot on the bull's horn and shoves. The beast just jerks his head, drools and digs his hoofs deeper into the dirt. Mrs. Glennie grabs a shovel. A couple of hefty whacks later, the bull plods into a livestock trailer.

This is crisp, clean writing: simple sentences, strong verbs, powerful images. This is style.

The final misconception, that style is mysterious and unattainable, is the hardest to discount. Because it is unique to the individual writer, style does seem to defy definition. But that doesn't mean it's mysterious. It means it's personal, idiosyncratic and distinctive. Far from being enigmatic, style is the sum of a series of good, solid decisions—many of them as basic as word choice or sentence construction—that a writer is aware enough, smart enough and experienced enough to make throughout the piece.

Style begins with accuracy and correctness and moves on to lively, original use of the language. It is always appropriate to the subject, the audience and the medium. Ultimately, it is the difference between a competent story and a memorable one.

Let's demystify style by examining some of its key components: liveliness, originality, rhythm and sound, and imagery.

LIVELINESS

Lively writing is not excitable, overwrought, exclamation-mark-studded prose, but clutterless composition that moves along at a good clip, involving readers or listeners and carrying them briskly from paragraph to paragraph. Like all components of style, liveliness depends not only on the way you use the language but also on what you have to say.

Style and substance go hand in hand. Your skills as an observer, interviewer and information gatherer net the raw material. Your skill as a writer transforms that material into vibrant prose. Here's how to make your writing lively.

Choose Verbs Carefully

Strong, precise verbs give energy to a sentence; weak, vague or overmodified verbs sap a sentence of its power. Instead of tacking on adverbs to clarify the meaning of a verb, spend time searching for the one right word.

Instead of	Use
talk incessantly	jabber, chatter, prattle
look into deeply	delve, probe, plumb
walk slowly	amble, trudge, saunter
eat quickly	gobble, wolf

Consider the abundance of simple, colorful verbs in this introduction to an article on our obsession with hair:

> We twirl, curl, cut and pluck it. We shave, brush, tint and wax it. We wash, braid and pomade it. We spend more than $2 billion a year pampering it and have more of it per square inch than a chimpanzee.

Use Intensifiers Sparingly

The adverbs *very, really, truly, completely, extremely, positively, absolutely, awfully* and *so* often add nothing but clutter. They show sloppiness of thought and generally add a too-colloquial tone to writing. Instead of intensifying a weak word, search for a strong, precise one.

Instead of	Use
very crowded	jammed
extremely thirsty	parched
really enthusiastic	zealous
awfully hot	scorching

When you've found a strong word, leave it alone. Don't rob it of its impact by unnecessarily intensifying it:

re~~al~~ly exhausted

extr~~em~~ely sweltering

tr~~ul~~y exceptional

Avoid Redundancies

Understand the meanings of words before you use them. *More equal, more parallel* and *most unique* are redundant expressions you can easily avoid if you pay attention to the meanings of *equal, parallel* and *unique.*

Edit to Remove Wordiness

Nothing destroys the vitality of prose faster, or as completely, as does verbosity, clutter, "purple prose," or bureaucratese. Each word, each phrase, each clause, each sentence should survive your rigorous editing process because it adds meaning, substance or color to the piece. Making every word count is the challenge. Review "Redundancy and Wordiness," "Vague Words," "Euphemisms and 'Fancy Words'" and "Jargon" in Chapter 11.

Use Active Voice

As you know from Chapter 8, active voice contributes to sharp, clear, vigorous sentence construction. In an active-voice sentence, the actor performs the action. In a passive-voice sentence, the actor has the action performed upon it. Passive-voice construction almost always weakens the verb and adds unnecessary words. It often sounds stilted and formal.

Use Present Tense

Present tense often allows the reader or listener to experience the story as it unfolds. When you use present tense as an element of style, you create a scene with urgency and immediacy. Consider this account, written in present tense, from a longer piece about a women's basketball team:

> B looks to pass but sees she's open, and it's her shot. She's outside the three-point line. She shoots with that high arc her father taught her in the driveway at home when he put trash cans in front of her, at age seven, and showed her how to loop the ball over the heads of the defenders.
>
> She watches her shot arc to the basket. It's in. She grins uncontrollably. No game face for her. A minute later, she makes an 18-footer, then sinks two free throws, then a lay-up. B isn't thinking anymore. When you're in a zone, the body takes over and the mind quiets. You need nothing but adrenaline and the ball.

Of course, the scene took place in the past. The writer is recounting it for the audience much later. But the present tense makes us feel as if we are there, courtside, watching the game. The scene is alive. Of course, not all stories can or should be told in present tense. Often past or future tenses are essential for historical accuracy. (Note that the sentence about B learning to shoot as a seven-year-old is in the past tense.) But the technique of narrowing the gap between audience and story by using present tense has many applications. Scene setting is certainly one of them.

Another is *attribution.* Using present tense to attribute quotations or present dialog in a story—*says* instead of *said,* for example—shows the immediacy of the comments, quickens the pace of the story and, in the case of conversational debate or opposing comments, shows the ongoing nature of the controversy. If a person said something yesterday, he or she would be likely to say the same thing today (unless, of course, we're talking about politicians).

No single element ensures lively writing. But if you use strong, precise language; rid your prose of clutter; stick with the active voice; and use, where appropriate, the present tense, your writing will be crisper, snappier and more inviting.

ORIGINALITY

Originality of style cannot be separated from originality of substance. If, as a thinker, observer, interviewer and cultural forager, you gather fresh material and come to novel insights, the written work you produce can be distinctive and original. When Health magazine columnist Mary Roach visited Florida to write about, of all things, Tupperware, she began her story this way:

> The Tupperware World Headquarters in Orlando, Florida, is a collection of long, low modular buildings, the sort of shapes you could easily stack one on top of another for just-right storage in your pantry, fridge or freezer, if that's the sort of person you were.

The playful tone and the unique visual image create an unusually enticing first sentence. This is what originality is all about: a novel vision translated into simple but imaginative language. This is style.

Or consider this wonderful sentence in the middle of a National Public Radio story about the emergency room of an animal hospital:

> In the examination room to the right of Dr. Cabe, a rust-colored dog is lying very still on the mirror steel table, its four legs splaying out at odd angles over the counter, as the couple who owns him hold one another, their faces colorless and almost round from crying.

The writing here is spare; the description precise, controlled and original. The writer could have described the faces of the dog owners as "pale and swollen from crying." But this is a familiar image, too familiar to touch the reader deeply. Faces "colorless and almost round from crying"—that's fresh and poignant. We'll talk more about description and scene setting in the "Show, Don't Tell" section later in this chapter. Let's concentrate now on originality of expression and on using language in fresh, vigorous ways.

Avoid Clichés

A *cliché*, by definition, lacks originality. It is a trite or overused expression or idea. It's the image or the phrase that springs immediately to mind. We've heard it before; we've read it before. We know it *like the back of our hand*. It's as *comfortable as an old shoe*. Get it? A cliché is someone else's idea, and the more it is used, the less power it has. As author Donald Hall writes, "When we put words together . . . we begin to show our original selves, or we show a dull copy of someone else's original." Note the following cliché-ridden remark from an economist offering the year's forecast. Unfortunately for the economist, the remark was quoted extensively in the national media!

Let's remember we climbed up the hill pretty darned quickly. We've had the rug pulled out from under us, but we've picked ourselves up, and maybe we can see the light at the end of the tunnel.

If the *light at the end of the tunnel* serves only to illuminate a cliché, it's not worth the trip, is it? The challenge is to use your imaginative and linguistic powers to create original expressions.

Play with Figures of Speech

Consider this simple but evocative simile in a New York Times story about a "spammer":

Damien Melle, who makes a living sending huge amounts of e-mail advertising over the Internet, works out of his home in this hard-scrabble Southern California suburb, in an office where the smell of fried food lingers like, say, unwanted e-mail in your in-box.

Or how about this metaphor in the middle of a quirky feature about a man who collects antique toasters and opened a toaster museum:

Ten years ago, Norcross' toaster obsession was unshaped dough on the breadboard of his life.

These writers are having fun. What grabs us when we read these two sentences, what makes us smile, is the unique vision, the odd or wonderfully apt comparisons. Similes are verbal comparisons that use *like* or *as* to announce themselves. Original similes have power, impact, even humor. Run-of-the-mill comparisons or clichés contribute nothing: *as black as night, as cool as a cucumber, hair like spun gold*. These comparisons lack verve and originality. Where is the imaginative stretch in *as black as night?* Night *is* black. What's the interesting comparison here? There is none.

Whereas similes are explicit comparisons using *like* or *as, metaphors* express a more direct comparison. Instead of stating that item A is "like" item B (a simile), a metaphor states that item A *is* item B. In the example above, the toaster collector's obsession was not *like* unshaped dough, it *was* unshaped dough.

When you attribute human characteristics, feelings or behaviors to nonhuman or inanimate objects, you are using a device called *personification*. Rushing to meet a deadline, you see the clock "staring" down at you. Clocks don't actually stare, of course. You've attributed a human quality to a mechanical object. You've personified the clock (albeit with a cliché!).

Below, author Susan Orlean has fun introducing Biff, who is a boxer (of the canine persuasion), in a New Yorker feature article:

Biff is perfect. He's friendly, good-looking, rich, famous and in excellent physical condition. He almost never drools. He's not afraid of commitment. He wants children—actually, he already has children and wants a lot more. He works hard and is the consummate professional, but he also knows how to have fun.

If you are thinking to yourself, "Figures of speech are fine for poets and novelists, but I'm a *journalist*," think again. As the examples in this section show, media writers can and do use literary devices to add zest to their writing. As information consumers become increasingly inundated with media messages, it becomes even more important to craft your message—be it a news story or advertising copy—in original and memorable ways, like using similes, metaphors and personification.

Play with Words

As the game began, the normally unflappable Shonely was flapped.

He's high on the scientists' favorite drug—discovery.

For millions of vegetarians, *beef* is a four-letter word.

These sentences, taken from news and magazine stories, show original language use. In the first, the word *unflappable* is turned on its head and transformed into a nonsense verb everyone can nonetheless understand. In the second, the writer plays with the reader's expectations. In the third, the cleverness turns on the accepted meaning of *four-letter word* as a curse word. All these plays on words are simple, straightforward, appropriate to the subject—and fun.

Word play need not be complicated or devastatingly witty to be effective. It need only be original, memorable and, of course, appropriate to the tone of the message.

RHYTHM AND SOUND

Words march to a beat. Long sentences move gently, liltingly, picking up momentum as they flow. Short sentences create a staccato beat. Repetition of words or phrases can add accent and meter. Sentence construction communicates. Words may have power, but words set in rhythmic sentences have clout. Let's examine six components of rhythmic sentence construction: repetition, parallelism, sentence length, fragments and run-ons, and the sounds of words.

Use Repetition

Purposeful repetition of words or phrases can add rhythm and grace to sentences. But, like all stylistic devices, it should be used sparingly. Too much repetition leads to boredom and clunkiness.

In the following magazine essay, note the repetition of *I don't mean:*

> I love the rain.
> I don't mean I grudgingly appreciate its ecological necessity. I don't mean I've learned to tolerate it. I don't mean I wait it out, flipping through the calendar to see how many more pages until the sun might break through. I mean I love it.

Repetition performs three stylistic functions here: It quickens the pace of the story by establishing a rhythm that pulls the reader from sentence to sentence; it creates smooth transitions; it sets up a mystery (What *does* the author mean?) that presumably the reader will want to read more about.

In tapping out a meter, repetition creates emphasis. The word or phrase you repeat assumes prominence and becomes a focal point. In the following passage, repetition of the word *gray* makes the point rhythmically and emphatically. Note too how the purposeful absence of commas in the second sentence helps the meter:

> At 5:30 on a December morning in Oregon you have to dig deep just to make it out of bed. About the best you can hope for this time of year is a slate gray dawn that lightens to a dove gray morning that slips into a pearl gray afternoon.

Repetition can be a powerful, dramatic and compelling technique. Perhaps that's why it is a favorite of speechwriters who want to add force to the spoken word. Some of the public speeches most remembered and most quoted depend on the element of repetition: Winston Churchill's compelling "We shall fight on the beaches . . ." World War II speech, which used the "We shall fight" litany to pound out both a rhythm and a message, or John F. Kennedy's "Let them come to Berlin" speech that repeated this sentence with increasing force.

Create Power with Parallelism

Parallelism is actually a kind of repetition, the repetition of grammatical patterns used to convey parallel or similar ideas. Parallelism is thus simultaneously a component of agreement (Chapter 6), coherence (Chapter

11) and style. Parallelism has the potential to create rhythm, emphasis and drama as it clearly presents ideas or action. Consider this long, graceful (and witty) sentence that begins a magazine article on sneakers:

> A long time ago—before sneaker companies had the marketing clout to spend millions of dollars sponsoring telecasts of the Super Bowl; before street gangs identified themselves by the color of their Adidas; before North Carolina State's basketball players found they could raise a little extra cash by selling the freebie Nikes off their feet; and before a sneaker's very sole had been gelatinized, Energaired, Hexalited, torsioned and injected with pressurized gas—sneakers were, well, sneakers.

First note the obvious parallelism of four clauses beginning with the word *before* and proceeding with similar grammatical patterns. Then note the parallel list of sneaker attributes: *gelatinized, Energaired* and so on. This is writing with pizzazz. It moves. It almost makes you interested in sneakers! Of course you noticed the nice bit of word play—the sneaker's very *sole*.

Vary Sentence Length

Short sentences are naturally punchy, emphatic and dramatic; long sentences are naturally lilting, rolling and restful. Sentence length communicates just as surely as do the words within the sentence. Writer Sallie Tisdale wanted a blunt, shocking first sentence for her controversial story on women's reproductive freedom. She chose two short, emphatic sentences linked by a semicolon to do the job:

> We do abortions here; that is all we do.

The power of both words and sentence length makes this compelling. On the other hand, consider this 52-word sentence about the creative work of an advertising copywriter who is the subject of an Esquire profile:

> He did some memorable commercials in the "McDonald's and You" series, including one marathon spot to launch the campaign, which ran on for as long as a travelogue and had grandparents and riverboats and airplanes and little kids in it, and made you proud, as well as hungry, to be an American.

Note how the sentence construction mirrors the idea the writer is communicating: the marathon length of the McDonald's commercial with its overabundance of kitsch images. The sentence is playful and seemingly endless (much like a commercial). It has rhythm. You can almost dance to it.

Take care with sentence length. If you construct a series of sentences of similar lengths, you run the risk of creating a plodding, deadening rhythm. If the sentences are all short, your prose may sound truncated and choppy, like a page from a children's book: "See the ball. The ball is green. Throw the ball." If the sentences are all long, the audience's attention may wander. Varying sentence length helps maintain interest while giving you the opportunity to use rhythm for drama and emphasis. For example, after the 76-word opening sentence of the sneaker article come these short, clipped constructions:

> They were flimsy things, canvas on the top and rubber on the bottom. The lowtops came in white or blue. The hightops came in white or black.

These punchy sentences provide a nice, rhythmic balance to the long, rolling introduction. Here's another example of using sentence length to communicate. Note the relatively long sentences followed unexpectedly by a short clipped sentence at the end.

> Duane Coop is standing 20 feet away from his practice target—a three-foot-diameter log with a painted red bull's-eye—throwing a two-and-a-half-pound, 32-inch double-bladed ax. The ax makes long, slow, end-over-end revolutions as it sails toward the target. Sprawled under the target, the family cat suns himself, listening without interest to the crack the six-inch blade makes as it slices into the log. The cat figures Duane won't miss. The cat's right.

Consider Fragments and Run-Ons

A fragment (an unfinished piece of a sentence) and a run-on (two or more complete sentences spliced together incorrectly) are grammatical errors. But certain grammatical rules can be bent by knowledgeable writers who are striving to achieve special effects. The rules against fragments and run-ons can occasionally be broken when you have a specific purpose in mind, when your audience (and editor) will stand for it and when the material warrants it. Advertising copywriters seem to be particularly fragment-happy. They can overdo it, creating choppy, confusing messages. On the other hand, they can use fragments effectively to create surprise and emphasis, as in this Nike ad that plays on a cliché:

> What does a 6'5", 270 lb. defensive lineman do for a workout? Anything he wants.

Anything he wants is a fragment. It's punchy, powerful, funny and appropriate to the subject and medium. It works.

Fragments can create excitement, set a quick pace and grab attention. Like short sentences—but even more so—they have a brisk, staccato beat. They can be tense, dramatic and emphatic. Here is the beginning of a dramatic passage about a writer's experience in Alaska:

It was 2 p.m. Thirty below. No wind. Totally dark. My boots squeaked on the dry, granular snow as I walked.

These fragments isolate and emphasize parts of the environment. They (excuse the wordplay) "freeze frame" certain details, the way a film editor would.

Unlike the staccato beat of fragments, run-ons can communicate a breathless, sing-song rhythm. Depending on the words and ideas, a run-on can quicken the pace with a giddy rush of words or slacken the pace with a languid, rolling motion. Consider this run-on sentence from a story by T. Coraghessan Boyle:

People can talk, they can gossip and cavil and run down this one or the other, and certainly we all have our faults, our black funks and suicides and wives running off with the first man who'll have them and a winter's night that stretches on through the days and weeks like a foretaste of the grave, but in the end the only real story here is the wind. The puff and blow of it. The ceaselessness.

That sentence lopes forward, layering idea on top of idea until the two fragments at the end abruptly change the pace.

Do remember that breaking grammatical rules is serious business, and that there's an important distinction between breaking a rule purposefully and breaking a rule because you don't know the rule. Before you use fragments or run-ons, ask yourself these questions:

■ Is the device appropriate to both the subject I am writing about and the medium I am writing for?

■ Is this device the best way to achieve the effect for which I am striving?

■ Does it work?

Don't use fragments or run-ons unless you can answer yes to all three questions. Even then use these techniques sparingly. Like all stylistic devices, they lose both meaning and impact when overused.

Listen to the Sounds of Words

"A sentence is not interesting merely in conveying a meaning of words; it must do something more," wrote poet Robert Frost. "It must convey a meaning by sound." Broadcast journalists and speechwriters learn to write for the ear, but print writers often pay little attention to the sounds of the words they choose. That's unfortunate because most readers *hear* the printed word in their minds as they read. Print writers should be writing for the "inner ear" of their readers. Words chosen and arranged for their sound, as well as their meaning, add style and verve to prose.

Our language is full of words that sound like what they mean. Onomatopoeic words like *crack, buzz, snap, bang* and *chirp* imitate the sounds they define. They are crisp, colorful and doubly descriptive. Note how the "liveliness quotient" increases when you choose a word for its sound:

Instead of	Use
complain	grumble, squawk, growl
fracture	smash, shatter, snap
talk (a lot)	jabber, yammer, chatter

Some words are not actually onomatopoeic, but their sounds add to their meaning. Words beginning with the "s" sound, for example, often communicate (by sound and meaning) a kind of unpleasantness: *sneer, smirk* and *snigger* are stronger, nastier words than *mock, deride* or *look askance*. *Entanglements* can be *complications, problems* or *puzzles*, or they can be *snarls* or *snags*. A dog can *dribble* or *drool*, or it can (even more unpleasantly) *slobber* or *slaver*. The meanings are the same; sound adds the extra dimension.

Words beginning with the "k" sound often communicate harshness or force. Politicians can have *power*, but when they have *clout* you know they're powerful. *Claws* seem more menacing than *talons*. *Carcass* or *corpse* is a harsher way of saying *dead body*. An ungraceful person is more *awkward* if described as a *clod*. In Chapter 11 we stressed the importance of choosing precise, accurate words. Here we are saying the writer striving for style ought to go one step further. Sound communicates. Look at both the meanings of words and their sounds.

IMAGERY

As writers, we are the eyes and ears of our audience. If we do our job well, we should be able to accurately re-create an event, a scene, a person, a moment in time for our audience. If we try harder, if we write with style, we can re-create in such vivid detail that our audience feels it has experienced what we write about. Including descriptive detail, showing rather than telling, and using quotations and anecdotes are all stylistic techniques that can bring the subject close to the audience.

Use Descriptive Detail

Remember the buildings at Tupperware headquarters that looked like plastic containers? Remember the faces of the couple—colorless and almost round from crying—whose sick dog lay on a steel table? This is descriptive detail. It can be a phrase, a sentence or the makings of an entire scene. Whatever it is, it focuses on particulars, illuminating details that help paint a picture. Consider this description of a house in a longer, biographical piece about its owner:

> Pancho's new house was on the outskirts of town on a half-acre of scorched dirt stubbled with desert weed and brush, an old wooden barn in back, a big, misshapen tamarisk tree in front. It was a squat, ugly, flat-roofed building made of chunks of rock set in concrete troweled over chicken wire. The rock was the color of dried blood.

The details, carefully observed and cleanly written, bring the reader closer.

Descriptive detail can capture an action, paint a scene or help re-create an event. Writer Joan Didion makes readers feel they are looking out the car window when she painstakingly describes this California scene. Note the purposeful use of fragments and manipulation of sentence length to control the rhythm of the passage:

> The way to Banyon is to drive west from San Bernardino out Foothill Boulevard, Route 66: past the Santa Fe switching yards, the Forty Wink Motel. Past the motel that is nineteen stucco teepees: "SLEEP IN A WIGWAM—GET MORE FOR YOUR WAMPUM." Past Fontana Drag City and the Fontana Church of the Nazarene and the Pit Stop A Go-Go; past Kaiser Steel, through Cucamonga, out to the Kapu Kai Restaurant Bar and Coffee Shop, at the corner of Route 66 and Carnelian Avenue. Up Carnelian Avenue from the Kapu Kai, which means "Forbidden Seas," the subdivision flags whip in the harsh wind.

This descriptive detail is plain and simple. There is a lot of it, but note how little Didion depends on adjectives. This makes the passage crisper and faster paced than it would be otherwise.

Show, Don't Tell

When you *tell* the audience something, you stand between the audience and the subject to offer judgments:

> The woman was energetic.

This "descriptive" sentence fails to describe. It summarizes the writer's conclusions instead of presenting details, images and concrete examples that would help readers draw their own conclusions. It *tells* rather than *shows*. Contrast it with this:

> She ran six miles, finished the report and faxed it to the home office, watered the garden, put in a load of laundry, worked on the speech she would be delivering next week and phoned three clients. Then she sat down to breakfast.

Now *that's* energetic. The details—not the writer's judgment—lead the reader to the conclusion.

Use Quotations

Lively, involving writing almost always includes people. The Wall Street Journal discovered this years ago and pioneered a style for writing about complex economic issues. It was deceptively simple: The stories all began with people whom the reader got to know through description and quotation. A complicated analytical piece on student loans would begin with one student and his story. Those who may have had little initial interest in reading a story about the economics of student loans would suddenly find themselves involved in the compelling personal story of a single student. Now hooked, they read on.

One way to bring people to the forefront of a story is to let them talk, to quote them. A *quotation* is a verbatim statement—the words between the quotation marks are the actual words spoken by the person being quoted. During the information-gathering process, media writers may listen to speeches; attend meetings and conferences; interview by email, telephone or in person; or stand in the background and listen to conversation. All the while they are scribbling notes or taping or both. When it comes to writing, they can be faced with pages and pages of quotations. How do they decide which to use and which to discard?

The first and most important consideration is *content*. Quoted material, like everything else the writer decides to include, should add to the audience's understanding of the message. The next consideration is *style*. Well-chosen quotations can be powerful elements in a story. They can:

- Bring the audience in direct contact with the person
- Capture and communicate a person's uniqueness
- Contribute to showing rather than telling
- Bring personality and passion to issues (even "dull" ones)
- Make a person—and a story—come alive

A well-chosen quotation clearly and vividly communicates something about the person. It is brief enough to hold the audience's interest. It expresses an idea that you, the writer, could not have said better. The last criterion is important. Sometimes people are long-winded; sometimes they go off on tangents. If you quote them (unless you are trying to show their long-windedness), you risk boring or confusing your audience. If the material is important enough to include, paraphrase it in your own words. Save quotations for strong, lively material.

But it's not just a quotation that can capture a person's uniqueness and enliven a story, it is how what was said was said—the context. The audience must be placed next to the person, must see and hear the person as he or she speaks. Consider the way quotations in context make this locker-room scene come alive:

> The coach takes a second to compose herself. Then, talking so softly that the girls have to lean forward to hear, talking as if she were speaking to herself and not to them, she says: "No one's going to promote us here but ourselves, ladies. We have to go out there and show them."
>
> She turns from them to put on the matching jacket to her taupe pantsuit. The girls are sprawled in their usual places, waiting now for her last word.
>
> "If we have to walk out of this place with a loss," she says, "I'm gonna puke."

Here's another example. Note how journalist Sally Quinn incorporates the contextual material as she goes along. Description and quotation work hand in hand as Quinn introduces the subject of her profile, then 90-year-old Alice Roosevelt Longworth:

> "I still," she muses, rapping her bony fingers against her graying head, "more or less have my, what they call, marbles," and she pulls her flowered shawl around her a little closer, throws her head back and laughs gleefully.

This quotation does everything a good quotation should. The reader can *hear* the subject talking.

Use Anecdotes

An anecdote is a short account of an incident, a "mini story" with a beginning, middle and end. An anecdote illustrates a key point in the story or highlights an important theme, offering detail and insight not possible any other way. It *shows* something the writer could have *told*, but in the telling would have weakened. Anecdotes can require a major expenditure of words, and media writers are often strapped for space or time. That's why it is vital to choose wisely, selecting that one moment that reveals, unmasks or captures some quintessential truth about the subject. Here is a well-told anecdote in a Columbia Journalism Review story that criticizes journalism education:

> "Now," Isaacs continued, slapping another article onto the overhead projector, "what's wrong here?"
> Everyone looked a little uncomfortable. *Is*es, *was*es and *has beens* clotted the prose.
> "Is?" someone offered.
> "Aside from that," Issacs said.
> The article under inspection concerned the disillusionment of male students at Vassar. Mainly, the piece consisted of a few limp quotes from a single source, a man who wished that he hadn't attended Vassar. Its chief weakness was that it was entirely devoid of interest, probably even to the person who wrote it. Like most of the other pieces, it emitted a sad, dispirited, homework smell.
> After a few unsuccessful guesses, the class gave up.
> "Look again," Isaacs said.
> We all looked again.
> "You don't see it?" Isaacs said.
> We didn't see it.
> "Vassar," he said.
> We were dumbfounded.
> "She's spelled *Vassar* with an *e.*"
> There was a little gasp of silence. It was true. *Vasser* stared out at us, accusingly.

This anecdote takes a while to relate, but it is worth every word. It has rhythm and pizzazz. It is fun to read—and it has a point. Imagine the writer just telling what the anecdote showed: Instruction about writing can sometimes be so picky as to miss the point. Or imagine a summary of the classroom interaction rather than the scene and story itself. All the oomph goes out of it. Well-told anecdotes are the product of superior observation and interviewing skills as well as sophisticated writing skills. They are tough to do, but very much worth the effort. Like descriptive detail, quotations and other "show, don't tell" techniques, anecdotes add zest to your writing.

WRITING WITH STYLE

"Rich, ornate prose is hard to digest, generally unwholesome and sometimes nauseating," writes E. B. White in the classic "Elements of Style." Lively, original, writing, on the other hand, is a delicately seasoned dish one can savor.

Writers spend their lives learning how to create irresistible prose. They read voraciously. They play with different ideas. They sweat the details. They make mistakes. But if they love their craft, and they love the language—and they have the patience and perseverance it takes—they *(you!)* can learn to write compelling, memorable prose.

 For online activities, go to the Web site for this book at *http://communication.wadsworth.com/kessler.*

CHAPTER 13

Sense and Sensitivity

In the days and weeks following the September 11, 2001, attacks on the World Trade Centers and the Pentagon, hundreds of Arab-Americans were verbally, and sometimes physically, harassed. The reason? They *looked like* those who had done great harm to the United States, and instant (and erroneous) judgments were made about their political beliefs and moral character based solely on their physical appearance. The enemy had an Arab face, ergo anyone with an Arab face was the enemy. This is hardly the first time something like this has happened in our large, diverse and, compared with much of the rest of the world, harmonious nation. African-Americans have for years protested "racial profiling," a usually unacknowledged practice by law enforcement agencies of targeting people based solely on race. Nor is this latest example the most egregious. That dubious distinction falls to the internment of 120,000 people with Japanese faces (three-quarters of whom were born, raised and educated in the United States) who were placed in barbed-wire encampments after the 1941 attack on Pearl Harbor because they too looked like the enemy.

We raise these points because they underscore the danger of seeing, treating and—for our purposes—*writing about* people not as individuals but as stereotypes: the terrorist Arab, the inscrutable "Oriental," the hot-tempered Latin, the mobster Italian, the miserly Jew. Stereotypes are never kind. They demean not only the group being stereotyped but also all of us who strive to live in a civilized society.

What can writers do about this? We all know how much words matter. Words shape our reality just as much as reality molds our language. Of course, words themselves do not cause nor can they solve the problems associated with unfair, discriminatory or hurtful treatment of others. But if we consciously or unconsciously use language that insults or that reinforces stereotypes, we support a world of prejudice and inequity. On the other hand, if we treat people fairly and sensitively—and individually—in our writing, we help create the kind of world in which most of us would like to live.

Unfortunately, this concept of treating people fairly with words has been much denigrated as "political correctness." Those who rail against it make jokes. Some of them are even funny: "Gee," they smirk, "should we start calling short people *height disadvantaged*? How about people who can't carry a tune? Let's call them *tonally challenged.*" It's certainly true that any reasonable concept can be taken to a ridiculous extreme, as these examples show. The point is that sensitive use of the language is a reasonable concept.

Language should help us appreciate and write about differences among people as it promotes fairness and tolerance. Choosing and using nondiscriminatory language is simple once you attune your sensitivities. Let's consider how to avoid several hurtful *"-isms"* in writing: sexism, heterosexism, racism, ageism and able-bodiedism.

SEXISM

Sexist language insults, stereotypes or excludes women. It treats men as the norm and women—although they make up 52 percent of the population—as the exception, the "other." Sexist language treats women as inferior to men, thus contributing to both the perception and the reality of inequality between the sexes. Inclusive, nonsexist, nondiscriminatory language, on the other hand, can help create a cultural and political environment that will not support existing inequities. Such language can also reflect the many positive changes that have already happened in the workplace and in the home.

Man Does Not Include Woman

One of the most insidious forms of sexism is choosing words meant to refer to both sexes that actually exclude women. We understand the word *man,* for example, to mean a male human being. When we use the same word to mean both male and female human beings (as in "Peace on earth, goodwill to *men*" or "All *men* are created equal"), we have a problem. How can one word simultaneously support two very different meanings? How can one word be both gender-exclusive (male only) and gender-inclusive (male and female)? It's like saying: "Sometimes when I write the word *apple,* I mean apple. But other times when I write the word *apple,* I mean apple and orange. I leave it to you to figure out which is the operative meaning." It's confusing.

When elementary school girls and boys were asked to draw pictures to accompany a hypothetical history textbook with supposedly gender-inclusive chapter titles like "Colonial Man" and "Democratic Man"—*man* here was supposed to be synonymous with *people*—they weren't confused at all: All the boys and just about all the girls drew pictures of men—male human beings, that is. We may talk about the generic, or gender-inclusive *man*, but in fact *man* is generally understood as male only.

Our language has a wide variety of inclusive words. When we mean "men and women," we have the linguistic capability to say so. General references should always be inclusive:

Instead of	Use
man, men	person, people
mankind	people
founding fathers	founders, forebears
gentlemen's agreement	informal agreement
manpower	work force
to man (verb)	to staff, operate

The Myth of the Generic *He*

Just as *man* cannot mean both men only and men and women both, so too *he* cannot refer to a male person at certain times and both genders at other times. When you use *he,* you communicate maleness, whether that is your intention or whether that is the reality. For example:

A lawyer must work for the best interests of his clients.

A child will gain confidence if he is allowed to make his own decisions.

Are all lawyers men? Are all children male? Use of *he* or *him* presumes and communicates gender exclusivity. The rule is simple: Never use *he* or *him* unless you are referring to a male. If you mean to be gender-inclusive, you have three choices:

1. When you must use a pronoun to refer to a noun of undetermined or inclusive gender *(lawyer, child),* recast the sentence with plurals. *They* and *them* are gender-inclusive:

Lawyers must work for the best interests of their clients.

Children will gain confidence if they are allowed to make their own decisions.

2. If sentence structure or meaning would be impaired by the plural, use *he or she, his or her,* or *him or her.* This construction can be a bit awkward—but not as awkward as excluding more than half the human race:

   A lawyer must work for the best interests of <u>his or her</u> clients.

3. Consider whether the pronoun is actually needed. Perhaps the sentence can be rewritten:

   A child will gain confidence if allowed to make independent decisions.

From Exclusive to Inclusive Job Titles

A few hundred feet from a group of workers cutting down roadside brush, you see a sign "Crew at Work." A decade ago you would have seen "Men at Work." Our language responds to societal change. Jobs that used to be male only and that carried male-only designations are now filled by both men and women. It is important to use the inclusive job designations. Here are some common ones:

Instead of	Use
mailman	mail carrier
policeman/policemen	police officer, police force
fireman	firefighter
newsman	reporter
businessman	businessperson, business executive, entrepreneur
salesman	sales clerk, sales representative
foreman	supervisor
congressman	senator, representative
chairman	head, presiding officer, chair
spokesman	representative, leader, spokesperson

Consistent Treatment of the Sexes

The consistency rule is simply stated and easily followed: When you write about men and women, treat them the same. If you refer to a man by last name only, do so for a woman. If you include such details as marital status, age and physical appearance when writing about a woman, make sure you would do the same if the subject were a man.

Let's say Mr. X is your state's new governor. Would you consider writing the following?

> With his flashing brown eyes and warm, gracious smile, Mr. X,
> grandfather of four, moved into the governor's mansion yesterday.

It sounds ridiculous, doesn't it? But, because of deeply entrenched sexism that allows women to be judged by different criteria than men, a *female* governor might very well be referred to in this way. How about a sports story in which the new female coach is described as a "curly-headed blonde?" Just imagine using a similar physical description for a male coach. It is laughable. If it would be inappropriate to offer this information about a man, it is equally inappropriate to offer it about a woman.

Contrary to the cliché, consistency is *not* the hobgoblin of small minds. It is a tool for nonsexist writing. Concern yourself particularly with consistency in the following five areas:

1. **Titles, names and references.** *Ms.,* which signals that the person named is female, but unlike *Miss* or *Mrs.* does not give information about her marital status, is the courtesy title of choice for women. It parallels *Mr.,* which signals maleness without marital status. When you use one, use the other. If you use titles like *Pres., Sen.* or *Rev.* to refer to a man, refer to a woman in the same way.

   Increasingly, publications are doing away with most courtesy titles, especially on second reference. In that case refer to both men and women by last names only, except when you are writing about a couple who share the same last name. Then full names, first names or courtesy titles (used equally for both halves of the couple) will provide clarity. Some writers like the informality of referring to people by their first names. If the story warrants such a tone and the publication allows for this style, first names should be used consistently for the sexes. Do not write "Mr. Dant and his assistant Patricia."

2. **Marital status and children.** Sometimes a person's marital or parental status is an appropriate and relevant piece of information that should be included in the story. Too often, though, women are defined by marital and parental status and men are not. Test yourself: If you would include the information for a man, do so for a woman. Consider this example:

> Seven Oaks real estate developer David Donnell has just completed
> a multimillion-dollar deal to refurbish the historic Smith Building.
> Donnell, father of three and husband of insurance executive Cheryl
> Miller, invested more than $1 million of his own money.

Sound ridiculous?

3. **Physical appearance.** Physical appearance may be completely appropriate to a story. Everyone wants to know how tall the new basketball center is (male or female). The overweight diet doctor, the business executive who wears Birkenstocks—these are all appropriate descriptions that add to readers' understanding. But too often women's clothes, bodies and mannerisms are described regardless of their relevance to the story. Women are not objects to be inspected and evaluated; they are, like men, subjects to be written about.

4. **Adding gender.** Most nouns in the English language are gender-inclusive: *writer, author, artist, scientist, doctor.* Treat them as such. Just as you do not need to insert *male* or *man* in front of these nouns when referring to a man in these positions, you should not insert *female* or *woman* when referring to a woman. You would probably never consider writing "*male* author Stephen King." Why then do we see such constructions as "*female* novelist Anne Rice"? Too frequently, writers add female gender to nouns that are actually gender-inclusive. The implied message: Only men are authors, artists, writers and so on. A woman is the rare exception. Of course if women—or men—are the exception, it's worth noting in some more sophisticated way.

5. **Equal treatment in word pairs.** When you pair men and women, make sure you choose equal words to refer to both sexes. Adult males and females are men and women; children are boys and girls.

Instead of	Use
man and wife	husband and wife
man and lady	man and woman; gentleman and lady
men and girls	boys and girls

HETEROSEXISM

Discriminatory or stereotypical language exists for any group whose physical appearance, behavior or beliefs vary from those in the mainstream. Homosexuals have traditionally had a difficult time swimming against that tide, and our language proves the point. We have dozens of words that insult and demean gay men and lesbians (*fag, fairy, dyke, butch*) and many more meant to tease and torment any woman who exhibits traditionally male behavior and any man who does not. Consider the simple ways writers can rid their language of bias and bigotry. Doing so has nothing to do with endorsing a "lifestyle" and everything to do with treating people as distinct human beings.

Not Everyone Is Heterosexual

Just as sexist language assumes maleness, heterosexist language assumes wholesale heterosexuality. But everyone is not heterosexual. Decades of research, both scientific and historical, have shown that about 10 percent of the population—now as well as centuries ago—is homosexual. That means one in ten of your readers (your colleagues, the writers you admire, the merchants you deal with) is gay. Because homosexuality has carried such a stigma in our society, until recently few gay men and lesbians have gone public with their sexual orientations. Thus many of us have grown up thinking of homosexuality as a rare occurrence. It isn't.

If you don't immediately assume the heterosexuality of those you write about, you can avoid awkwardness (for example, asking an interview subject why he or she never married) and surprise (upon learning, for example, that a "feminine-looking" woman is a lesbian).

A Person Is Not His or Her Sexual Orientation

Although a person's sexual orientation may be vital to the story—a profile of a gay activist, a church and its homosexual parishioners—many times it is not. If you would not consider writing "The company owned by heterosexual entrepreneur Leslie Morse, . . ." why include information about homosexual orientation? Even worse is such wording as "an admitted homosexual" (as if the person were admitting to a heinous offense) or a "practicing homosexual" (do we ask heterosexuals whether they "practice," too?).

Beware of Stereotypes and Exceptions

Homosexuals cannot be stereotyped any more than can heterosexuals. They are all ages, all races and ethnicities, all religions. They live in different parts of the country and are employed in all occupations. Some are single; others live with lifelong partners. Some have children; others do not.

It is important to understand this diversity for two reasons. First, it will help you avoid thinking of (and describing) a gay person as a "type." Second, and probably more important, it will help you guard against making a point of characteristics that don't conform to the "type," calling special attention to such "oddities" as the lesbian with long hair or the gay man with children. The assumption behind these observations is that all lesbians look a certain way, that all gay men live a certain kind of life. Do all heterosexuals look and act alike?

RACISM

Those Americans of African, Asian, Native American or Hispanic descent—that is, those who look noticeably different than Americans of European descent—are the most obvious victims of racist attitudes, behavior and speech. Racism can affect every part of their lives, from where they live to the medical services they receive, from the quality of their education to their self-esteem and self-image. Racism is a problem of enormous proportion in the United States (and worldwide). Americans of various European ancestry labor under the burden of ethnic stereotypes as well: the arrogant German, the dumb Pole, the drunken Irish. There are more than enough negative and hurtful slurs to go around.

It is unlikely that you would demonstrate overt racism in your writing. But it *is* likely that your judgment would be affected by the long-standing and pervasive stereotypes that exist in our society. Regardless of your own personal goodwill, you assuredly harbor some prejudices; you undoubtedly "see" people through the filter of stereotype. Here is how to make sure your language is prejudice-free.

Don't Identify People by Race

Do not identify a person's race or ethnicity unless it is a relevant or an interesting part of the story. If someone is the first of his or her racial or ethnic group to achieve a certain goal, that fact may be newsworthy (although those "first who" stories can quickly become trite). But if you would not normally identify a person as being "white" in a story, do not use racial identity at all. Relatively few situations require the inclusion of race.

Don't Reinforce Stereotypes by "Exceptions"

Language can reinforce racism by treating people as exceptions to stereotypes, which is just as demeaning as using the stereotype itself. For example, making it a point to call an Italian-American "respectable and law-abiding" implies that most are not, thus reinforcing the Mafia stereotype. Writing that a Mexican-American is "hardworking and even-tempered" implies that Mexican-Americans in general are indolent and volatile. The negative stereotype is embedded in the "positive" attributes.

Avoid Using "Non-Whites"

Eurocentrism—using white, European culture as the norm—is evident when you refer to people as "non-whites." Why describe people by what they aren't? Would you call a 25-year-old a "non-teen"? Would you call a brunette a "non-blond"? Of course not. Be particularly careful when using the word *minority* as well. In a growing number of U.S. cities, in the state of California and in the world in general, *whites* are the minority.

Be Sensitive to Group Names

Be aware of what members of various racial and ethnic groups call themselves and want to be referred to publicly. These names change with the times. Early in the 20th century, black Americans were called "coloreds" and pressed hard to be called the more respectable term *Negro*. In the 1960s *black* and *Afro-American* were the terms of choice. Today many people prefer *African-American,* a term consistent with how we refer to other Americans of international heritage (*Asian-Americans,* for example). Indians are generally referred to as *American Indians,* as *Native Americans* or as members of particular tribes or confederations. Those descended from Spanish-speaking cultures might be referred to as *Chicano(a), Latino(a), Hispanic* or, more specifically, by country of origin *(Cuban-American, Mexican-American).*

Given that the word *minorities* may be factually inaccurate and that *non-whites* is Eurocentric, the search continues for a more sensitive aggregate term. *People of color* is a current favorite, although some people find it less than acceptable. It may also be somewhat less than accurate, as olive-skinned whites of Mediterranean ancestry can be more "colorful" than some people of color. Rather than lump together a variety of racial and ethnic groups and hunt for a single descriptor, it seems preferable to simply list the groups themselves.

AGEISM

Codger, fogy, fossil. Geezer, duffer, coot. Hag, nag, bag, crone. Senile citizens. Our language is not kind to older people.

Older people are feeble, frail and forgetful, crabby, creaky, constipated and curmudgeonly. These are the stereotypes, and they are not only insulting, they are largely inaccurate. The vast majority of older people live healthy, productive and independent lives. The active, alert, involved older person is the rule, not the exception.

As people live longer and as that huge demographic blip known as the baby boomers move through middle into old age, the numbers of older Americans will increase dramatically. At the turn of the 20th century, one in 16 Americans was 60 or older. Today it's one in six. Within the next decade and a half, it will be one in four. It is past time for writers to learn how to deal accurately and sensitively with older people.

Few writers would actually use any of the offensive terms listed at the beginning of this section, but many might find the stereotypes pervading their writing in more subtle ways. Generally, ageist language reinforces damaging stereotypes by expressing great surprise over those who do not conform to them.

She is still vigorous at 70.

His mind is still sharp at 75.

The implication is that most 70-year-olds lack vigor and that most 75-year-olds are senile. If you refuse to accept the inaccurate stereotypes, you will avoid making insulting statements about "exceptions."

Although our society (and its language and images) is unkind to older people of both genders, more women than men may be victimized by ageist language. The stigma of aging is greater for women, who, throughout their lives, have traditionally been evaluated more by what they look like than by who they are. A gray-haired or balding man of 65 might be thought of and described as "distinguished" or "at the height of his powers." A gray-haired woman of 65 is rarely thought of or described in such complimentary terms.

Ageism exists on both ends of the life span. Teenagers are irresponsible, inarticulate, hormone-driven slackers—or so goes the stereotype. That accounts for the ageist singling out of "responsible" and "thoughtful" teens, as if they were the surprising exception rather than, in fact, the rule.

To write sensitively and accurately about people in any age group, question your assumptions and reject stereotypes. Write about people as individuals, not as representatives of, or exceptions to, their age group.

"ABLE-BODIEDISM"

No, that is not a word, and we are not suggesting that it should be! *Able-bodiedism* is a term we've coined here to stand for language discrimination against people with disabilities. Tens of thousands of Americans have physical or mental disabilities, some of which limit their activities and impair their performance, some of which do not. A disability does not necessarily "disable" or make one a "disabled person." Some disabilities simply don't affect one's work. (Is the writer in a wheelchair a "disabled writer"?) Other disabilities, in fact, create new abilities.

When writing about people with physical or mental limitations, ask them how they want to be referred to. Also keep in mind this vital rule: People are not their handicaps. People *have* handicaps (limits, impairments, different abilities). Never write:

Arthur Thomas, an epileptic . . .

The handicapped children . . .

Assuming it's relevant, write instead:

Arthur Thomas, who has epilepsy . . .

The children, who all have handicaps . . .

THE -*ISMS* GOLDEN RULE

All this advice boils down to one rule: Write about others as you would want them to write about you. You see yourself as an individual who may be male or female, old or young, fat or thin, black, brown or white. Consider the stereotypes for each one of these categories. Are you the stereotype or are you a distinct individual? You are, of course, an individual. See—and write about—others with the same regard for and sensitivity to *their* individuality. This is not a matter of being "politically correct." It is a matter of being human.

 For online activities, go to the Web site for this book at *http://communication.wadsworth.com/kessler.*

Topical Guide to Grammar and Word Use

Sometimes you just need to know the answer *now. Who* or *whom? Its* or *it's? Among* or *between?* And what was that comma rule again? You're in the midst of writing, and you want to keep focused, or you're on deadline and every minute counts.

This is why we offer Part 2.

The brief alphabetical listings that follow are not meant to take the place of the longer discussions we offer in Part 1. But they can point you in the right direction—fast.

Style guides can be iffy. Some are too authoritarian—"my way or the highway" manuals that refuse to see language as a living, changing organism. Others are so permissive that they take anarchy to new levels, accepting so many definitions and uses of words that the proper meanings and nuances are lost. Still others are downright eccentric, reflecting the peccadilloes of their authors rather than the logic of usage.

We hope our guide falls into none of these categories. We strive to be both respectful of legacy and open to change. Although we recognize—and celebrate—the dynamism of our language, we also urge caution in adopting trendy (and often sloppy) spoken standards. We hope this guide will challenge you to maintain proper usage and meaning as you seek new and creative ways to improve your expression.

-able/-ible endings   These *suffixes* (endings to root words) can be frustrating. Why do we have accept*able* on one hand and imposs*ible* on the other? There really is no good reason. But it may help to remember that *-able* endings are more common and that in most cases the *able* suffix is attached to complete root words (*change* + *able* = *changeable*). As Chapter 10 emphasizes, imprinting—seeing the words in print many times over—is necessary to avoid the wrong suffix choice. See p. 128 for that list of pesky words.

active voice/passive voice   *Voice* refers to the form of a verb. When the subject of the sentence *performs* the action of the verb ("She wrote the story"), the verb *(wrote)* is in the *active voice*. If the subject *receives* the action ("The story was written by her"), the verb *(was written)* is in the *passive voice*. The active voice is always stronger and more direct than the passive voice. Use it unless you have a good reason not to—for example, when you need to stress the receiver of the action rather than the performer or when the performer is unknown. See Chapter 8 for a complete discussion of voice.

adjective   This part of speech is a "finishing touch" for a noun or a pronoun. As a modifier, the adjective describes, limits and adds important detail. The writer's biggest challenge with adjectives is choosing the right ones—in meaning, nuance and tone—for the job. Adjectives are the hue and chroma of our writing. The spectrum of color they can provide is almost limitless.

adverb   Adverbs generally answer *how, why* and *when*. Strong adverbs work in tandem with descriptive verbs to create powerful imagery. In expressing matters of degree, time, place and manner, however, the adverb can modify not only verbs but also adjectives and other adverbs. Like the adjective, the adverb must be chosen carefully and applied precisely. Remember that not all adverbs end in *ly!* (That would be much too simple.)

adverse/averse   Although these adjectives sound alike, they have distinct meanings. *Adverse* means "unfavorable or hostile":

The senators did not expect such <u>adverse</u> reaction to the education amendment.

If you want to describe someone's reluctance to do something, you should use *averse:*

The president was not <u>averse</u> to vetoing the bill.

affect/effect   A pox on this pair! Misusing one for the other is one of the most common usage errors. It's true that the words sound alike, but they are most often different parts of speech. *Affect* is almost always a verb that means "to influence or to pretend to have." *Effect* is almost always a noun that means "result." For example:

AF–AL

The new program will <u>affect</u> millions of welfare recipients.
> (*verb:* "to influence")

The prisoner <u>affected</u> a carefree manner.
> (*verb:* "to pretend to have")

The senator questioned the <u>effect</u> of the welfare cutback.
> (*noun:* "result")

But just to make life interesting, *effect* is occasionally used as a verb in formal writing to mean "to bring about," and *affect* can be a noun in very narrow usage to denote certain behavior in psychology:

Top management <u>effected</u> some personnel changes.
> (*verb:* "to bring about")

Flat <u>affect</u> is a sign of depression.
> (*noun:* "psychological state")

Neither of these is common enough to worry about in your everyday writing.

***-aholic* endings**   Here is proof that language indeed lives. Through slang usage *aholic* tacked onto a word has come to mean "one obsessed by," as in *workaholic* and *chocaholic*. Presumably these new words owe their existence to *alcoholic*. But instead of taking the accepted suffix *ic*, meaning "of or pertaining to," from the root word *alcohol*, the creators of these new words stole (and misspelled) another syllable and a half. That this linguistic configuration makes no sense bothers only purists. The rest of us enjoy new words with distinct meanings.

aid/aide   Don't be fooled: *Aides* ("assistants") give *aid* ("help, assistance") to their bosses. *Aid* also can be a verb, but *aide* can be only a noun. So, constructions such as "the president's aide" and "giving aid and comfort to the enemy" are correct.

all/any/most/some   These pronouns can take singular or plural verbs, depending on the meaning. If the word carries the meaning of "general amount or quantity," it is singular:

<u>All</u> of the contraband <u>was</u> seized at the port.

Some of his testimony was stricken from the record.

If you can read "individual and number" into the sentence, the plural verb should be used:

All of the children were safe.

Have any of their relatives been notified?

See p. 68 and the entry for *none*.

allude/elude   These meanings shouldn't elude you. If you are making an indirect reference to something, you *allude* to it (if you want to mention it directly, you *refer* to it):

The candidate alluded to his opponent's prison record.

Elude is your choice if you mean "to escape or to avoid detection."

The fugitive eluded the search party for two weeks.

among/between   These two prepositions will probably always confuse us. You may have learned this rule: *Among* relates to more than two persons or things, and *between* applies to only two. But it's not that simple. A truer guide is this: If there is a definite relation involved, *between* is preferred, no matter what the number:

Between you and me, this business will never succeed.

Negotiations have broken down between the government mediator, autoworkers and management.

Among is properly used where there is no explicit relationship stated and when distribution is stressed:

The handbills were passed out among the crowd.

The reward money was divided among the four families.

One other point about these prepositions: Remember that if they are used in a simple prepositional phrase, their objects and personal pronouns will be in the objective case. For more on this, see p. 80.

antecedents   Often hiding in a sentence like a serpent in tall grass, an *antecedent* is the noun to which a pronoun refers. A clear connection between the antecedent and the pronoun is necessary for the sentence to make sense and read well. But sometimes the antecedent of a pronoun is unclear, and writers may have problems with agreement between the antecedent and the verb. In the following sentences, proper antecedents are underlined:

Sarah is one of those <u>people</u> who never <u>require</u> more than four hours' sleep.

(Why is the antecedent *people* instead of *one*? Because the sentence tells us that there is more than one person who can get by on that amount of sleep, that clause needs a plural verb, as people *require*.)

Zane is the <u>only one</u> of the finalists who <u>isn't</u> nervous.

(In this sentence only one finalist isn't nervous, hence the singular verb.)

Gerry's <u>theory</u> is intriguing, but not many of his colleagues agree with <u>it</u>.

(The pronoun *it* properly refers to the antecedent *theory*. The intriguing theory, not Gerry, is the focus.)

a number of/the number of   The intended number of these phrases depends on the article. If the article is *a*, the meaning is plural:

<u>A number of</u> students <u>are</u> going on the field trip.

If the article is *the*, the meaning is more indefinite (or is seen as a unit) and therefore is singular:

<u>The number of</u> West Nile virus cases <u>has</u> increased recently.

These phrases illustrate an easy-to-remember tip about subject–verb agreement: If the phrase or word denotes "a general amount or quantity," the verb is singular; if the phrase or word denotes "a more definable number of individuals," the verb is plural. See p. 65.

anxious/eager   Why so many people use *anxious* when they mean *eager* we don't know. *Anxious* implies fear and worry:

The mayor says she is <u>anxious</u> about the outcome of the election.

If you are stimulated and excited at the prospect of doing something, you are *eager* to do it:

Lizzie is <u>eager</u> to start third grade.

You can only be anxious about something; you cannot be anxious *to do* that thing.

appositive   This is a word, phrase or clause that renames or adds information about the word that precedes it. Words in apposition have a side-by-side relationship. They are important to identify because they have some bearing on punctuation and case decisions. For example, a *restrictive* appositive is one that is essential to the meaning of a sentence and thus requires no commas:

> My friend <u>John</u> helped write headlines while his friend <u>Susan</u> finished
>   (appos.)   (appos.)
> the design.
> (A comma would not be correct after *friend* because *John* and *Susan* are essential to the meaning of the subject.)

A *nonrestrictive* appositive still has a side-by-side relationship, but its meaning is not essential to the sentence. It must be set off by commas:

> Mullins, <u>a proven clutch player</u>, has a secure place on the roster.
>   (appos.)

as if/like These are *not* interchangeable. *As if* acts as a conjunction and introduces a clause:

> It looks <u>as if</u> it will rain.

Like, a preposition, takes a simple object and cannot introduce a clause:

> It looks <u>like</u> rain.

Some grammarians say that *like* may evolve into a conjunction. (We're not holding our breath.)

as/than Because *as* and *than* can be both prepositions and conjunctions, case selection may be tricky. If these words are used as conjunctions, it is most likely to make comparisons. If so, the nominative case of the pronoun is needed:

> There's no one more handsome <u>than</u> he.
> ("Than he is handsome" is understood as the second clause.)

However, *as* and *than* can also be prepositions:

> Why did you pick Beth rather <u>than</u> her?

Obviously, no comparison is being made here. The pronoun following the preposition must be in the objective case.

as well as This phrase, which connects a subordinate thought to the main one, can cause agreement problems between subject and verb. Remember that the main subject—not any word or phrase parenthetical to it—controls the number and the person of the verb:

> The <u>house</u>, as well as its contents, **<u>was</u> destroyed** in the early-morning fire.

Similar parenthetical phrases are *together with, in addition to* and *along with.* You'll find it easier to isolate the true subject of the sentence if you set off these phrases with commas. See p. 65.

bad/badly   Don't feel bad if you use these words badly! *Bad* is an adjective. In linking-verb constructions in which you want to describe the subject, *bad* is the correct choice:

The mayor said he <u>felt</u> <u>bad</u> about the library budget defeat.
        (l.v.)(adj.)

This sentence describes the mayor's state of being, not his physical ability to feel. When you describe some quality of the verb instead of the subject, you use the adverb *badly:*

The prime minister <u>took</u> her defeat <u>badly</u>.
        (verb)   (adv.)
(*Badly* describes the verb *took,* not the noun *prime minister.*)

because of/due to   You should always use *because of* when matching cause to effect. It is used when the writer can ask *why* in a sentence:

The stock market crashed <u>because of</u> panic selling.

Due to should be used only in a linking-verb construction. *Due* is an adjective; its preposition *to* relates to the condition of a subject:

The increase in the cost of burritos is <u>due to</u> soaring prices of jack cheese.

Note that you can't ask *why* in this construction, but you can in the next, which is why *because,* not *due to,* is correct:

<u>Because of</u> the budget crunch this year, no new positions will be created.

beside/besides   *Beside* means "next to" or "at the side of." *Besides* means "in addition to":

The nervous guard stood <u>beside</u> the visiting dignitary.
        (next to)

<u>Besides</u> Jake and me, only Erik knew of the escape plan.
(in addition to)

Remember that simple objects of these prepositions take the objective case.

bi-/semi- *Bi-* means "two," and *semi-* means "half." *Bimonthly* means every two months; *semimonthly* means twice a month. If you mean something that happens twice a year, use *semiannual* rather than *biannual,* even though the dictionary recognizes both. That will avoid confusion with *biennial* (something that happens every two years). Note that the prefixes *bi* and *semi* are hyphenated only when the word that follows them begins with an *i* or is capitalized.

both/few/many/several These indefinite pronouns always take a plural verb. See p. 66.

brand names/trademarks These are business-created words that have not fallen into generic usage. Do you really want to refer to a specific product, or do you just want to mention the process? If you want to mention the process or the generic name, avoid brand name reference. Do not write, for example:

The spy <u>xeroxed</u> all the documents.

For one thing *Xerox,* a registered trade name, isn't a verb; the spy can *photocopy* the documents, but he or she can't *xerox, canonize* or *savinize* them. Other examples are *Scotch tape* (a brand of cellophane tape), *Coke* (one of many cola beverages), *Mace* (a brand of tear gas) and *Kleenex* (a brand of facial tissue). All brand names and trademarks should be capitalized.

bureaucratese/jargon Jargon has changed our language—but not for the better. These words and phrases, used by government workers, scientists, doctors, computer programmers and a host of other professionals, usually do more to obscure than elucidate. For example, you no longer measure the effect of deficit spending on a budget; you ascertain how the program will *impact fiscal planning.* You no longer evaluate things; you *effect a needs assessment.* A heart attack becomes an *M.I.* (myocardial infarct). When these professionals talk to one another, their language may be both efficient and precise. But when journalists write for broader audiences, this specialized language does not work.

but *But* is most frequently a conjunction, connecting words and phrases of equal rank and implying a contrast between those elements. It almost always requires a comma between the clauses it separates:

The commissioners approved the budget, <u>but</u> they vetoed a room tax provision.

But also can be a preposition meaning "except":

Everybody <u>but</u> me went to the party.

Note that the objective case is required for the pronoun.

Can *but* be used to begin a sentence, like the conjunctive adverb *however?* But of course—if you don't overdo it.

can/may   Please preserve the distinction between these words. *Can* denotes ability, and *may* denotes possibility and permission. If your sentence is in the form of a question, *may* is almost always your choice:

> May I go to the exhibit?
> (Permission, not ability, is the question.)

> Do you think I can win this election?
> (Do I have the ability to win?)

Some stylebook authorities have thrown in the towel on the interchangeability of *can* and *may,* but we're not willing to give up the fight. Postscript: Remember that *may* can also express possibility.

> I may buy that new boat we've been talking about.

case   *Who* or *whom? Us* or *we?* Understanding *case* helps us make these grammatical choices. The three cases are nominative, objective and possessive. Certain pronouns change their form to accommodate a change in case. Nouns change only in their possessive case. See Chapter 7.

censor/censure   These words have different meanings, pronunciations and spellings, so what's the confusion? Perhaps it's because the meanings are interrelated. You can *censor* materials by screening, changing or forbidding them.

> The press officer censored all dispatches from the battle lines.

You generally can *censure* only people—by condemning them or expressing disapproval of their actions.

> The senators censured their colleague because he attempted to censor a staff report.

These words can also be nouns. So, you can have an "official government censor" as well as a "resolution of censure."

chair/chairperson   We believe the term *chairman* unfairly and incorrectly assumes maleness of that position. It is one of many such terms in our language (for example, *policeman* and *businessman*). For years authoritative dictionaries have referred to *chair* as "a person who presides over a meeting" and "an office or position of authority." A person—man or woman—can chair a meeting or be a program chair. It assumes nothing but the position itself. *Chairperson* seems a bit more awkward to us, but it may be what an organization chooses to call its leader. The person's official title should be used. See Chapter 13.

clause   This is a group of words that contains both a subject and a verb. An *independent clause* (otherwise known as a *sentence*) expresses a complete thought and can stand alone. A *dependent clause* has a subject and a verb, but the meaning is incomplete, and the clause cannot stand alone. See p. 48.

CL-CO

clutter   This is the excess baggage that obscures clarity in writing. Mercilessly prune from your prose these flabby words, redundant phrases or just plain longwinded expressions. Sharpen those clippers—and review Chapter 11.

collective nouns   They look singular *(jury, herd, committee)* but obviously imply plurality. Or they can look plural *(athletics, politics)* but imply singularity. What's a writer to do? Here's the answer: If the noun is considered as a whole, the verb and associated pronouns are singular:

The committee is meeting today.

Politics is a dirty business.

If the unit is broken up or considered individually, the plural verb is required:

The herd of cattle have scattered.

The senator's politics are changeable.

See p. 67.

collision   This is a violent contact between *moving* bodies. An accident between a moving car and a stationary telephone pole is not a collision; it is a *crash*. But an oil tanker might *collide* with a frigate. In a more figurative sense, ideas, opinions and, yes, words can collide.

colon   This punctuation mark (:) introduces thoughts, quotations, examples or a series. Capitalize matter following a colon only if it can stand alone as a sentence:

Her parting words inspired them for years: "You must think outside the box."

Besides cartooning, Charles Schulz had one great passion: hockey.

comma splice   Also known as *comma fault,* this is a mistake by the careless writer who joins two independent clauses without either a coordinating conjunction or a semicolon:

> The council approved the resolution, the mayor vetoed it the next day.
> (The sentence lacks the conjunction *but* or a semicolon between clauses.)

> He enjoys reviewing movies, however, he says he can't waste his time on "trash like this."
> (Presence of the conjunctive adverb *however* requires a semicolon between clauses—that is, between *movies* and *however.*)

In short sentences the comma splice has received the blessing of most grammarians. "You'll like her, she's a Leo" can survive without a conjunction or a semicolon. An accomplished writer who does not want the harsh stop of a semicolon to slow the meter of a sentence might employ the comma splice as a stylistic tool. But, like the sentence fragment, the comma splice should be used sparingly—and only by writers who know what they're doing.

compared to/compared with   These are about as interchangeable as American and European voltage. When you liken one thing to another, you *compare* it *to:*

> She <u>compared</u> writing a book <u>to</u> running a weekly marathon.

When you place items side by side to examine their similarities and differences, use *compared with:*

> The study <u>compared</u> last winter's rainfall <u>with</u> winter rains for the previous 10 years.

As you can see, the use of *compared to* is figurative and metaphorical. *Compared with,* on the other hand, is statistical rather than creative.

complement/compliment   Both of these terms can be nouns or verbs. *Complement* means "that which completes something, supplements it or brings it to perfection." *Compliment* means "an expression of praise or admiration." So, a necklace might *complement* a blouse, but you would *compliment* the wearer on the necklace.

compose/comprise   *Compose* is not as direct as *comprise.* Something is *composed of* other things (made up of); however, one thing *comprises* (takes in, includes) other things. The following are correct usages:

> His salad dressing was <u>composed</u> of olive oil, balsamic vinegar and puree of turnip.

Her speech <u>comprised</u> four major themes.

As you can see from the last example, the whole *(speech)* comprises the parts *(themes)*. A whole is never *comprised of* the parts. That would be the same as saying (nonsensically) that "the whole is included of its parts." But *comprise* is not a word we would use more than occasionally. Sometimes it just doesn't sound right!

compound modifiers   These are two adjectives or an adverb joined with an adjective to modify a noun. Often a hyphen is needed to join these modifiers to make the meaning clear:

<u>mud-splattered</u> bike

<u>well-intentioned</u> meaning

<u>hard-driving</u> perfectionist

Modifiers do not require a hyphen if they are preceded by *very* or an *-ly* adverb. These adverbs obviously modify what follows, and there is no mistaking their connection:

<u>very energetic</u> teacher

<u>highly motivated</u> student

Don't string together too many modifiers in the name of description and economy. You'll simply get clutter.

conjunction   The *conjunction* links words, phrases and clauses; if used properly, it provides both logic and rhythm to a sentence. Note, for example, how the conjunction *and* provides a sense of parallelism or equality to a clause:

The border guard quickly stamped the passport <u>and</u> cheerfully directed the tourist to the nearest town.

But (a great conjunction—it provides a contrast or shows a lack of unity) note how the conjunction *and* can be used improperly when it links obviously unequal or unrelated elements in a sentence:

She came in early to work this morning, <u>and</u> she is buying a new car.

Also see *as if/like* and p. 41.

conjunctive adverb   Words like *however, therefore* and *nevertheless* may look like conjunctions, but they are really adverbs. Why is this distinction important? It's because conjunctive adverbs need a semicolon—not a comma (as conjunctions)—to link sentence parts. For example:

The book is a best seller; <u>however</u>, I find it pretentious and poorly written.

See p. 43.

continual/continuous *Continual* means "repeated or intermittent." *Continuous* means "unbroken":

Must I suffer these <u>continual</u> interruptions?

The parched hiker imagined a <u>continuous</u> line of canteens stretched across the barren horizon.

convince/persuade If you think these words are identical in meaning, we're just going to have to persuade you that they're not. We'll do that until you're convinced! To begin with, people do not *convince* others of anything; that action is called *persuasion:*

His doctor <u>persuaded</u> him to take a vacation.

To be *convinced* is to be secure in a decision or a principle. It is always an adjective, not a verb:

He was <u>convinced</u> nothing was wrong.

If a person attempts to persuade another and is successful, the first person is considered persuasive. Obviously the argument has been convincing. The process is to persuade; the hoped-for result is to be convinced. Got that now? Convinced? Or do you need to be persuaded?

dangling modifiers A modifier "dangles" when it does not directly modify anything in the sentence. For example:

Facing indictment for insider trading, the grand jury called her to testify.

The participial phrase *facing indictment for insider trading* has nothing to modify. The first referent we see is *grand jury*. But that can't logically be the referent. Poor sentence construction has buried the true referent—the person who is facing indictment. The sentence needs to be rewritten:

Facing indictment for insider trading, Stewart was called by the grand jury to testify.
(Yes, this is in the passive voice, but the recipient of the action, Stewart, is more important than its initiator, the grand jury.)

Dangling modifiers most often occur at the beginnings of sentences. Although they tend to be *verbals* (participial phrases, gerund phrases and infinitive phrases), appositives, clauses and simple adjectives can dangle as well. The test is whether the person or thing being modified by the word,

CO-DA

phrase or clause is in the sentence. Dangling modifiers destroy coherent thought. Rewrite or revise the sentence to include the missing referent. See p. 139.

dash   An enticing piece of punctuation because of its informality, directness and drama, the dash (—) is often used excessively and incorrectly. Media writers should consider routinely using commas, colons and parentheses and saving dashes for special occasions. The two main uses of the dash in media writing are as follows:

1. To create drama and emphasis at the end of a sentence:

   The film was beautifully photographed, superbly acted, expertly directed—and excruciatingly boring.

2. To clearly set off a long clause or phrase that adds information to the main clause:

   "Little Nicky"—Adam Sandler's one big mistake—was a box-office bomb.

Remember that excessive use robs the dash of its power.

data and other foreign plurals   Many English words have their roots in Latin; some are derived from Greek. Some of these words conform to singular–plural rules unlike our own. *Data, media* and *alumni* are common Latin plurals. Magazines are one *medium;* radio and TV are broadcast *media.* The word *alumni* presents its own complications: A group of men and women who have graduated from a school are *alumni;* one male graduate is an *alumnus;* one female grad is an *alumna.* And to be perfectly correct, a group of female grads would be *alumnae.* The Greek words *criteria* and *phenomena* are plural. Their singulars are *criterion* and *phenomenon.*

   Data can be a confusing word. It's plural but is most often considered a unit—a collective noun—and should take a singular verb:

   Your <u>data</u> <u>is</u> invalid.
   (unit)
If the sense of *data* is individual items, however, use a plural verb:

   The <u>data</u> <u>were</u> collected from seven tracking sites.
   (individual items)

dependent clause   Although it contains both a predicate and a subject, a *dependent clause* does not express a complete thought and cannot stand alone as a sentence. Dependent clauses rely on main clauses for their completion:

Because the tax levy failed
(dep. clause)

Because the tax levy failed, the library will cut its hours.
(dep. clause linked to indep. clause)

Recognizing dependent clauses will help you (1) avoid fragments (treating dependent clauses as if they were complete sentences) and (2) vary sentence structure. Place the dependent clause in front, in the middle or at the end of the main clause to vary sentence structure. See p. 48.

DI

different from/different than   For those who take comfort from edicts, here's one: Use *different from* and you will never be wrong. If this leaves you wondering why *different than* exists, join the ranks of contentious grammarians who have been arguing this point for years. Unless you're interested in delving into the nether regions of structural linguistics or semantic compatibility, consider using *different than* only when it introduces a *condensed clause* (a clause that omits certain words without loss of clarity).

Open-meeting laws are different in Illinois than [they are] in Oregon.
(condensed clause)

In general, however, play it safe with *different from*. So the previous example would read:

Open-meeting laws in Oregon are different from those in Illinois.

differ from/differ with   Politicians who *differ from* (are unlike) others may not necessarily *differ with* (disagree with) each other. Although these phrases express contrast, they are not interchangeable. When you mean two items are dissimilar, use *differ from*. When you mean items are in conflict, use *differ with*:

The competing proposals did not significantly differ from one another.

The developers differed with the zoning committee.

discreet/discrete   Yes, it's true—both of these words are adjectives, and both are pronounced the same. But they do have discrete meanings! *Discreet* means "prudent or careful," especially about keeping confidences, as in this sentence:

The therapist was less than helpful, but at least he was discreet.

Discrete means "distinct or separate,"as in this sentence:

The two words have discrete meanings.

disinterested/uninterested   A *disinterested* (impartial) observer may be *uninterested* (lack interest) in the situation, but the words are not synonymous.

drug   A *drug* is any substance used as medicine in the treatment of a disease. Headline writers have made this word synonymous with *narcotics,* a particular group of sense-dulling, usually addictive drugs. All narcotics are drugs; all drugs are not narcotics. Be precise when using these words. To avoid confusion (and the possibility of libel), use *medicine* when referring to a substance used to treat a disease or an injury.

each/either/neither   When used as subjects, these three pronouns always take singular verbs:

Each is responsible for his or her own equipment.

Neither of the defendants was found guilty.

When these words are used as adjectives, the nouns they modify always take a singular verb:

Either answer is correct.

Neither candidate speaks to the issues.

either . . . or/neither . . . nor   Called *correlative conjunctions,* these word pairs (along with *both . . . and, not so . . . as* and *not only . . . but also*) connect similar grammatical elements in parallel form:

He can either pay the back taxes or risk a jail sentence.

Correlative conjunctions also pose agreement problems. When a compound subject is linked by a correlative conjunction, the subject closest to the verb determines the number of the verb:

Neither the researcher nor her assistants were available for comment.

When the subject closest to the verb is singular, you must use a singular verb. The construction is grammatical but sometimes graceless:

Neither the assistants nor the researcher was available for comment.

Avoid awkwardness by placing the plural subject next to the verb. See p. 67.

elicit/illicit   These two words may sound alike, but the similarity stops there. *Elicit,* a verb, means "to bring out or draw forth." *Illicit,* an adjective, means "illegal or unlawful."

His illicit behavior elicited strong community reaction.

eminent/imminent These are both adjectives, but they describe very different qualities. *Eminent* means "distinguished or prominent":

The eminent scientist Linus Pauling won two Noble Prizes.

Imminent means "about to occur" or "impending":

The Internet company is facing an imminent takeover.

Note that there is one *m* in *eminent* and two in *imminent*. Don't ask us why!

EM-FE

enormity/enormousness These words are not synonymous. *Enormity* means "wickedness." *Enormousness* refers to size.

The enormity of the September 11 attacks is still difficult to comprehend.

The enormousness of the budget deficit has staggered even the most nimble politicians.

exclamation mark Expressing strong emotion or surprise, the exclamation mark (!) is rarely used in journalistic writing. Its use is almost always limited to direct quotations. Remember to place the exclamation mark inside the quotation marks:

"I'll kill you when this is over!" the witness screamed at the prosecutor.

farther/further One of these years, you probably won't have to worry about this bothersome duo. *Farther,* say grammarians, is on the way out. But language often changes slowly, and the distinction between these two words will be with us for a while. Use *farther* to express physical distance; use *further* when referring to "degree, time or quantity":

The commission wants to extend the boundaries farther south.

The commission will discuss the boundary issue further.

feel Save this overused word to refer to the tactile or emotional; do not use it as a synonym for *think* or *believe.*

fewer/less This is a much-abused pair, but the distinctions are simple: When you refer to a number of individual items, *fewer* is your choice; when you refer to a bulk, amount, sum, period of time or concept, use *less:*

Fewer doctors result in less medical care.

At Data Corporation fewer than 10 employees make less than $50,000 per year.

In the latter example, we are not talking about individual dollars but a sum (amount) of money.

fragments   An unfinished piece of a sentence, a *fragment* may be a single word, a phrase or a dependent clause. It may lack a subject, a predicate, a complete thought or any combination of the three. Whatever form it takes, whatever element it lacks, a fragment is not a grammatical sentence and should not stand alone. Fragments can be rewritten to include subject, predicate and complete thought; incorporated into complete sentences; or attached to main clauses. See p. 52 and the *sentence* entry.

FR-GE

Now you know the rule. Here's the loophole: Fragments, when used purposefully by skillful writers, constitute a stylistic technique. With their clipped, punchy beat, fragments can create excitement and grab reader attention. But this stylistic device must be appropriate to both subject and medium and should be used sparingly.

gender-specific references *(he/she)*   Language reflects culture and beliefs. When a society changes, we believe language ought to keep pace. We are speaking not of faddish words or slang expressions but of the way language treats people. The language in the following sentences is no longer an accurate reflection of our society:

> A <u>nurse</u> ought to be attentive to <u>her</u> patients.

> A <u>state legislator</u> has a responsibility to <u>his</u> constituents.

In these sentences we see outdated gender stereotypes—nurses are all female, legislators are all male. From a grammatical point of view, the problem is choosing a referent *(she, he, him, her, his, hers)* that reflects reality rather than presuming maleness or femaleness of a neuter noun. Because the singular neuter pronoun *(it, its)* cannot refer to a person, we have two grammatical options if we want to avoid gender stereotyping:

1. Use both the masculine and the feminine pronoun when referencing a noun that could refer to either sex:

> A <u>nurse</u> ought to be attentive to <u>his or her</u> patients.

2. Change the neuter noun to the plural and use plural neuter pronouns *(they, them, their)*:

> <u>State legislators</u> have a responsibility to <u>their</u> constituents.

In your effort to treat both sexes fairly in language, don't fall prey to easy (and incorrect) solutions that accept errors in agreement:

<u>Everybody deserves</u> to make it on <u>their</u> own.

This may be well-intentioned, but it is grammatically incorrect. Two solutions are obvious:

<u>Everybody deserves</u> to make it on <u>his or her</u> own.

<u>All people</u> deserve to make it on <u>their</u> own.

See Chapter 13.

hanged/hung   The verb *hang* is conjugated differently depending on the object of the hanging. The conjugation *hang, hung, hung* refers to objects: **HA–HO**

The portrait <u>hung</u> in the museum foyer.

The conjugation *hang, hanged, hanged* refers to people (executions or suicides):

He <u>hanged</u> himself in his prison cell.

Homophones, homonyms and homographs   If you're looking for more reasons to love the English language—or lose patience with it—look no further. *Homophones* are words that sound the same but are spelled differently and have unrelated meanings, like *fair* and *fare, alter* and *altar,* and *whose* and *who's.* If your vocabulary comes from spoken English (TV, for example) rather than written English (books), these words can mess you up. Spell-checkers won't help, as the incorrectly used words are, in fact, spelled correctly. Read! *Homonyms* are words that sound the same, are spelled the same but—oddly—have completely different meanings, as in *stable* (horse stall) and *stable* (unwavering). As if this were not enough, *homographs* are spelled the same but—maddeningly—are pronounced differently (and have different meanings), as in *bow* (in archery) and *bow* (of a ship).

hopefully   Possibly the single most abused word in our language, *hopefully* means "with hope." It describes how a subject feels *(hopeful).* Therefore, this sentence would be correct:

<u>Hopefully</u>, Roy Paul opened the mailbox, looking for the check.

Hopefully—regardless of what you may hear or read—does not mean "it is hoped that." Therefore, the following sentence is incorrect:

<u>Hopefully</u>, the check will arrive.

The check is not "hopeful." *Hopefully* does not describe anything in the preceding sentence. It is, in fact, a dangling modifier. People have so thoroughly abused *hopefully* in conversational language (making it synonymous with "it is hoped") that the abuse is now part of our written language. For correctness, precision and clarity, respect the real meaning of the word. If you mean "it is hoped," write that.

hyphen   Whereas the dash creates a dramatic break in a sentence, the workhorse *hyphen* creates a typographical bridge that links words for several purposes.

1. It joins compound modifiers unless one of the modifiers is *very* or an *-ly* adverb (compound modifiers are two or more adjectives or adverbs that do not separately describe the word they modify):

    a <u>well-educated</u> soldier
    (hyphen needed)

    the <u>newly appointed</u> ambassador
    (*-ly* adverb, no hyphen needed)

2. It links certain prefixes to the words that follow. One basic guideline: If the prefix ends in a vowel and the next word begins with the same vowel, hyphenate (except *cooperate* and *coordinate*). It's best to check a dictionary or stylebook on this rule because exceptions abound. Some examples:

    the <u>pre-election</u> suspense

    but:

    a <u>precursor</u> of the election results

3. It links words when a preposition is omitted:

    score of <u>10-1</u>
    (preposition *to* omitted)

    closed <u>June-August</u>
    (preposition *through* omitted)

See p. 113.

-ics words   Words ending with the suffix *-ics (athletics, politics, graphics, acoustics, economics)* can create problems with agreement. Although their final *s* makes these words *look* plural, they can be either singular or plural depending on meaning. If the word refers to "a science, art or general field of study," it is treated as singular and takes a singular verb. If the word refers to "the act, practices or activities" of the field, it takes a plural verb:

<u>Politics</u> is an impossible career.
(the field of politics, singular)

His <u>politics</u> seem to change every year.
(the practice of politics, plural)

Some *-ics* words do not carry both meanings. *Hysterics*, for example, always takes the plural because it always refers to "acts and practices."

if I were English uses the subjunctive mood to express a nonexistent, hypothetical or improbable condition. That "mood" calls for what itself seems grammatically incorrect—a plural verb with a singular subject. But these sentences are grammatically correct:

IF

<u>If I were</u> the world's richest person, all medical care would be free.

If you want to express a condition that is possible, however, it would be correct to say:

<u>If I was</u> president of this company, these accounting scandals would cease.

if/whether These conjunctions are not interchangeable. *If* means "in the event that," "granting that" or "on the condition that." It is often used to introduce a *subjunctive clause* (a clause that expresses a nonexistent, hypothetical or improbable condition):

<u>If</u> the team wins tonight, the coach will cut off all his hair in celebration.
(in the event that)

<u>If</u> the volcano were to erupt again, thousands of lives would be threatened.
(hypothetical condition)

Whether means "if it is so that," "if it happens that" or "in case." It is generally used to introduce a possibility:

He wondered <u>whether</u> he should attend the briefing.
(if it is so)

<u>Whether</u> he wins or loses, this will be his last campaign.
(introduces possibilities)

For the sake of precision and conciseness, use *whether*, not *whether or not*. The *or not* is implied:

<u>Whether</u> the schools will remain open depends on the fate of the budget levy.

impact   This noun means a "collision" or a "violent or forceful striking together." Unfortunately, writers use *impact* when they really mean something much less forceful, such as *effect* or *influence.*

> When her car hit the guardrail, the impact threw her from the vehicle.
> (correct)

> We can't predict what impact this report will have on future negotiations.
> (misuse—better to use *effect* or *influence*)

Unfortunately, *impact* has also fallen prey to those who toss it around as a verb ("The televised debates *impacted* the election") or an adjective ("federally *impacted* areas"). The only thing that can be impacted is a tooth, and that's unpleasant enough.

imply/infer   Misused far too often, these verbs are not interchangeable. *Imply* means "to suggest or hint." *Infer* means "to deduce or conclude from facts or evidence."

> When she implied that Smith was unethical, the search committee inferred that she had an ax to grind.

indefinite pronouns   Because indefinite pronouns (*anyone, everyone, few, some,* etc.), don't always specify a number, they can cause agreement problems. Here are a few rules to follow:

■ When used as subjects, *each, either, anyone, everyone, much, no one, nothing* and *someone* always take a singular verb.

■ Acting as subjects, *both, few, many* and *several* always take a plural verb.

■ Pronouns such as *any, none* and *some* take singular verbs when they refer to a unit or general quantity. If they refer to amount or individuals, they take a plural verb:

> Some of the shipment was delayed
> (general quantity)

> because some of the workers were on strike.
> (individuals)

See pgs. 64–68.

independent clause   An independent clause contains a subject, a predicate and a complete thought.
This is an independent clause:

> Tom replied to his critics,

This is not:

charging that they were funded by his political opponents.

See p. 48.

-ing endings   A common suffix, *ing* is added to a verb to create the present progressive form ("She is running for office.") or a verbal ("Running for office requires tenacity."). It can also be added to a noun, creating a verbal (a gerund) that gives the noun a sense of action. For example, *parenting* is the action of being a *parent.* Although *"inging"* a noun may occasionally create new words with distinct meanings, it can also be unnecessarily trendy. Language should change in response to culture and not merely for the sake of change. Consider this example:

IN

The boss believes in gifting her staff during the holidays.

This is an ugly, awkward construction. Use new *-ing* words sparingly and only when they capture a unique meaning without damaging the rhythm and sound of the language. See also the *-ize* entry.

in/into   These prepositions are not interchangeable. *In* denotes location or position. *Into* indicates motion.

The photographer was already in the courtroom when the star
                                    (location, position)
witness was ushered into it.
                    (movement)

Regardless of current slang, *into* should never be used as a substitute for "involved with" or "interested in." This colloquial use is not only sloppy but also weak and ambiguous:

For the past year, she's been into swimming.
(ambiguous slang)

She's been swimming a mile a day for the past year.
(improved)

initiate/instigate   At our own instigation, we have initiated an investigation of this troublesome pair. When you mean that a deluded artist began or originated a contest, for example, it is *not* correct to write this:

He instigated the first tofu sculpture contest.

Instead, he *initiated* (began) it. This would be a proper use of *instigate:*

She instigated the recall movement in the school district.

In this case she did not begin the investigation—she pressed for it.

insure/ensure/assure Please be assured: These words are different! If you limit the meaning of *insure* to activities of insurance companies, you'll always be correct.

Tom wants to <u>insure</u> his house for earthquake and flood damage.

Ensure, on the other hand, means (in a noninsurance sense) "to guarantee" or "to provide something":

She promised to <u>ensure</u> the safety of the reporters.

What about *assure?* Used correctly, this verb speaks directly to a person, to give him or her confidence in a promise:

She <u>assured</u> them that their insurance coverage was adequate.

invoke/evoke Probably because both words contain -*voke* from the Latin root *vocare* (to call), these very different words are often used interchangeably. *Invoke* means "to appeal to or call forth earnestly." *Evoke* means "to produce or elicit" (a reaction, a response) or "to reawaken" (memories, for example):

When the speaker <u>invoked</u> God, he <u>evoked</u> a strong reaction from the audience of atheists.

irregardless Strike this silly word from your vocabulary! *Regardless,* which means "without regard for" or "unmindful of" is what you're after. The *less* suffix creates the negative meaning. When you mistakenly add the *ir* prefix, you create a double negative.

its/it's This odd couple creates more grammatical scandal than any other word pair. Okay, once and for all: *Its* is the possessive form of the neuter pronoun it. Do not confuse this with *it's,* which is a contraction for *it is* or *it has:*

The committee reached <u>its</u> decision yesterday.
(neuter possessive)

"<u>It's</u> going to be a close vote," said Mayor Smith.
(contraction of *it is*)

By the way, please use *it* or *its*—not *she* or *her*—when referring to nations or ships:

Somalia is reviewing <u>its</u> paltry military options.

The S.S. Howdy Doody sails for <u>its</u> home port at Disney World this afternoon.

See p. 33.

***-ize* words**   An occasionally useful suffix, *ize* has been employed since the time of the ancient Greeks to change nouns into verbs *(final/finalize, burglar/burglarize)*. But the "-ization" of words has now reached epidemic proportions. We've been alarmed at the growing use of *"incentivize,"* for example. Writers interested in the clarity, precision and beauty of language need to take precautions. Tacking *-ize* onto nouns often creates useless, awkward and stodgy words. Will it get worse? Will we soon read:

The president announced a plan to <u>soldierize</u> the U.S. Postal Service.

The agency may <u>permanentize</u> its position by <u>routinizing</u> its appointment procedures.

"Verbizing" nouns is dangerous business. The result is often tongue-twisting, bureaucratic-sounding clutter. Before you use an *-ize* word, check your dictionary. Make sure the word has a unique meaning, and pay attention to its sound.

IZ-LA

kind of/sort of   Conversationally we use *kind of* and *sort of* to mean "rather" or "somewhat":

It's <u>kind of</u> [a somewhat] cloudy today.

I'm <u>sort of</u> [rather] tired.

But casual usage and clear, precise written language are two different things. So—please restrict your use of *kind of* and *sort of* to mean "a species or subcategory of," as in:

Tom is the <u>kind of</u> executive who takes no prisoners.

In many cases you can eliminate the problems posed by *kind of* and *sort of* by avoiding the words themselves:

Tom is an executive who takes no prisoners.

lay/lie   *Lay,* as transitive verb form, *always* takes a direct object; *lie,* an intransitive verb, *never* takes a direct object:

The sheriff <u>laid</u> the <u>smoking gun</u> on the bar.
               (dir. obj.)

The Seychelles <u>lie</u> in the <u>Indian Ocean</u>.
               (prep. phrase)

Be careful not to confuse *lie* and *lay* in the past tense. The past tense of *lie* is *lay:*

He finally <u>lay</u> down for a long winter's nap.

See p. 20.

lend/loan   In spoken language the distinction between these two is almost nonexistent. But rather than worry about the differing niceties observed by various editors, play it safe: Use *lend* as a verb and *loan* as a noun. The one exception currently favored by most experts is *loan* as a verb in financial contexts:

The bank <u>loaned</u> the troubled firm $45 million.

This would be an appropriate use of *lend:*

Please don't <u>lend</u> him your car for the weekend; you'll be sorry!

less than/under   Do not use *under* unless you mean "physically beneath." If you mean "a lesser quantity or amount," use *less than:*

The county budget is <u>less than</u> $80 million.

The stolen money was found <u>under</u> the bridge.

Also see entries for *fewer/less* and *more than/over.*

linking verbs   A *linking verb* connects a subject to an equivalent or related word in the sentence. That word—a predicate noun, a predicate pronoun or a predicate adjective—refers to the subject by either restating it or describing it. The principal linking verbs are *be, seem, become, appear, feel* and *look.*

She <u>is</u> a best-selling novelist.
(*Novelist,* a predicate noun, restates subject *she.*)

It <u>is</u> he.
(*He,* a predicate pronoun, restates the subject *it* and stays in the nominative case.)

He <u>feels</u> bad.
(*Bad,* a predicate adjective, describes the subject *he.*)

Note that *badly,* an adverb, cannot be used in this construction. See the entry for *bad/badly* and p. 21.

literal/figurative   Considering these two words have opposite meanings, it's amazing that writers will substitute one for another. *Literal* means "word for word" or "upholding the exact meaning of a word":

This is a <u>literal</u> translation of the Celtic myth.

Figurative, on the other hand, means "not literal; metaphorical, based on figures of speech":

Figuratively speaking, she's on top of the world.

may/might   Time to split the proverbial hairs! Both of these verbs indicate possibility, as in "I *may* go to Sara's party tonight," but some usage experts contend that *may* indicates a stronger possibility than *might*. So what to do? Our advice is to stick with *may* unless the possibilities for action are extremely remote:

I might as well be the man in the moon.

median/average (mean)   *Median* is the middle value in a distribution of items, the point at which half of the items are above and half are below. *Average* is the sum of a group of items divided by the number of items in the group. *Mean* is statisticians' talk for average. Statistically, *average* and *mean* are virtually synonymous.

MA–NO

Number of years spent on death row by prisoners of state X:

Prisoner A	18	Prisoner D	10	Prisoner G	6
Prisoner B	14	Prisoner E	7	Prisoner H	6
Prisoner C	10	Prisoner F	6	Prisoner I	4

The *median* years spent on death row is 7; that is, half of the prisoners spent more than 7 years in jail, half spent less. The *average* (or *mean*) number of years spent on death row is 9; it is the sum of all the years (81) divided by the number of prisoners (9).

more than/over   Like *less than* and *under,* these words are not interchangeable. Do not use *over* unless you are referring to a spatial relationship. For figures and amounts, the correct phrase is *more than:*

More than 100 jets flew bombing and support missions over the desert.

none   This indefinite pronoun often causes agreement problems. Use a singular verb when *none* means "no one or not one." When *none* means "no two, no amount or no number," use a plural verb. Don't be fooled by a plural prepositional phrase—*none* is the subject:

None of the suspected rioters was arrested.
(not one rioter)

None of the taxes were paid.
(no taxes—no amount)

See the entry for *indefinite pronouns* on p. 68.

numerals   Many media organizations have specific style rules concerning numerals. Check first. In the absence of other guidelines, follow these rules:

1. Spell out whole numbers below 10: three, seven.

2. Use figures for 10 and above: 14, 305.

3. Spell out fractions less than one: two-thirds, three-quarters.

4. Spell out *first* through *ninth* when they indicate a sequence: She was first in line; the Ninth Amendment. Use figures for 10th and above.

5. Spell out numerals at the beginning of a sentence. The only exception is a calendar-year date.

There are also many guidelines for ages, percentages, fractions, election returns, monetary units, dimensions, temperatures and other specific cases. The Associated Press Stylebook is a good, comprehensive reference.

occur/take place   Contemporary usage favors this distinction: *Occur* refers to "all accidental or unscheduled events"; *take place* refers to "a planned event":

The power outages <u>occurred</u> within an hour of each other.

Opening ceremonies <u>take place</u> at 2 p.m.

off of   Be wary of prepositions that enjoy one another's company. You may be practicing grammatical "featherbedding"—having two do the job of one. *Off of* is one of those redundant, bulky constructions. *Off,* all by its lonesome, suffices.

<u>Get off</u> [of] my back!

Driscoll <u>walked off</u> [of] the stage and never performed again.

one of the/the only one of the   Having a verb agree in number with its subject is not difficult—once you identify the proper subject. When the subject is a pronoun (*who* or *that,* for example) and it refers to a noun elsewhere in the sentence, the task is somewhat challenging. Subject–verb agreement then depends on determining the correct antecedent. For *one of the/the only one of the,* follow these rules:

1. In *one of the* constructions, the relative pronoun refers to the object of the preposition of the main clause, not the subject:

NU-ON

<u>Easter</u> is one of the best <u>ballplayers</u>   <u>who</u>   <u>have played</u> the game
(subj.)   (obj. of prep.)(pron.)(verb)
in the last 50 years.
(If you examine this sentence, you will see that *Easter* is not the only ballplayer who has played the game in 50 years. We are talking about *many players* who *have* played the game in that period.)

2. In *the only one of the* constructions, the relative pronoun refers to the subject of the main clause:

<u>Mayor Drinkwater</u> is the only one of the candidates <u>who</u>
(subj.)   (pron.)
<u>has opposed</u> the tax referendum.
(verb)
(There were no other candidates who opposed this referendum. The antecedent clearly is *Drinkwater*.)

parallel structure   When you place like ideas in consistent grammatical patterns, you create *parallel structure*. This consistency among elements gives order to writing and helps make the message clear. Parallelism also creates balance, symmetry and sometimes rhythm in a sentence. Common errors in parallelism include mixing elements in a series, mixing verbals and switching voice. See p. 71.

paraphrase   This is a form of editing—a correct and concise summary of a direct quotation that may be too long or semantically awkward to use. Accuracy is the key here.

According to Mayor Johnson, the proposed zoning change will block the city's plan to develop more low-income housing.

Be sure that is what the mayor said—and meant.

parentheses   Writers should use parentheses sparingly because the reason for their use—to provide additional information or an aside for the sentence—is generally contrary to brief, crisp writing. For those rare occasions when you do use them, here is a simple rule concerning punctuation: Put the period *inside* the parentheses only if the parenthetical material is a complete sentence and can stand independently of the preceding sentence:

Tom is not the accountant who was indicted in the dot-com scandal.
<u>(It was his partner Sam, who goes to trial next month.)</u>

If these conditions are not met, the period goes outside:

The mourners chanted, "Vaya con Dios" <u>(Go with God)</u>.

See p. 116.

passive voice   This is an odd, generally ineffective and occasionally deceptive construction in which the subject of the sentence is actually the recipient of the verb's action. It adds words while diminishing clarity. Doesn't seem like a good idea, eh? Note the difference in directness and conciseness between these two examples:

The accounting scandal dubbed "Restatementgate" by journalists and commentators will be investigated by the Senate subcommittee.
(passive, in two constructions)

The Senate subcommittee will investigate the so-called Restatementgate accounting scandal.
(active)

There are, however, suitable occasions for passive voice. See Chapter 8.

PA-PR

people/persons   Some editors contend that a "group" should be referred to as *people*, but "individuals" should be called *persons*. So, what is the scale of acceptable use for *persons* (three? six?)? Put another way, when does a particular number of *persons* become *people?* We suggest you save yourself the headache! There are more pressing decisions in life. So— if you are referring to "one individual," you are referring to a *person:*

She's a wonderful person, don't you think?

If you are referring to "more than one," use *people:*

Twelve people were arrested this morning in the jaywalking sting operation.

possessives   Chapter 7 discusses in detail the formation of possessives. This point, however, deserves emphasis: Possessives of personal pronouns are not the same as subject–verb contractions. Remember that the personal pronoun possessives *(my, mine, our, ours, your, yours, his, her, hers, its, their, theirs)* do *not* require an apostrophe. See also the entry for *its/it's.*

preposition   This is a handy part of speech that links phrases and neatly ties a sentence into a coherent package:

The burglar was hiding behind the freezer.
(The preposition *behind* begins the prepositional phrase.)

Although a preposition can occasionally introduce a clause, it almost always precedes a phrase. When that phrase contains a pronoun, that pronoun must stay in the objective case:

Don't lay the blame on us reporters for this spate of bad news.

Avoid burdening a sentence with an unnecessary series of prepositions:

Dr. Flagranto followed his victim <u>through</u> the French doors <u>next to</u> the solarium, <u>with</u> the evil intent <u>of</u> murder <u>on</u> his mind.

Let prepositions enhance a sentence—don't let them drain the power of the verb!

preventive/preventative   Why in the world use *preventative?* It uses two extra letters and still means preventive! It's pretentious, that's why. Practice preventive language arts—avoid overweight, unnecessary words.

principal/principle   As a noun *principal* is "someone who is first in rank or authority," such as the principal of a school. As an adjective *principal* still means "first in rank or authority," such as the "principal reason for the levy's defeat." *Principle,* however, is only a noun. It means "a truth, doctrine or rule of conduct," such as "an uncompromising *principle* of honesty."

PR

prior to   What's the matter with using *before? Prior to* is stuffy and falsely formal.

pronoun   It means, literally, "in place of a noun." Unlike nouns, pronouns change their form in the possessive (for example, *their* for *they*), which is why pronoun possessives don't need apostrophes (and that's why the subject–verb contraction *it's* is *not* a pronoun!). Careless writers often position their pronouns indiscriminately, causing problems with antecedent identification:

<u>Pentagon briefers</u> tried to explain the field reports to the <u>journalists</u>, but it was apparent that <u>they</u> were hopelessly confused.
See the problem? Be sure that antecedents are clearly identified.
See p. 69.

proved/proven   Use *proved* as the past participle of the verb *prove:*

The district attorney <u>has proved</u>, beyond a reasonable doubt, the guilt of the defendant.

Proven, although cited by some dictionaries as an acceptable alternate for the past participle, is preferred in journalistic style as an adjective only:

The district attorney has a <u>proven</u> track record for convictions.

In a linking-verb construction, use *proven* if it takes the role of the predicate adjective:

The district attorney's success is <u>proven</u>.
(*Proven* is not part of the verb. It is an adjective that modifies *success.*)

quotation marks   A common question about quotation marks is where to place other marks of punctuation with them. Here is a brief recap:

1. Periods and commas always go inside the quotation marks.

2. Question marks and exclamation marks go inside *if* they are part of the quoted material.

The most common error in quotation mark punctuation is in placement of the question mark. Two examples show its correct placement:

> The senator asked the company president: "Can you honestly tell me that your baby food formula has never caused the death of a child in a Third World country?"
>
> (The question mark belongs inside because it is part of a quoted question.)

> What did you think of "Austin Powers"?
>
> (The entire sentence is a question; the quoted movie title is declarative.)

QU-RE   See Chapter 9.

quotation/quote   *Quotation* is a noun. *Quote* is supposed to be a verb. In newsrooms, however, *quote* is often used as a noun. ("Get me some good quotes for this piece. It's dying of boredom.") Journalists are economical souls. In general, remember to quote only the good quotations!

real/really   We're *really* serious about these differences—they are *real*. Please remember: *Real* is an adjective, and it modifies nouns; and in the case of the linking-verb construction previously, it can modify a pronoun. *Really* is an adverb; it modifies adjectives. So, just to be clear: It would be really bad writing to say that you write "real well." Got it?

rebut/refute   It's easier to rebut a statement than to refute it. When you *rebut* a statement, you contradict it or deny it. But that doesn't mean you have conclusively proved the truth of your position. When you *refute* a statement, you *have* proved that you are correct. Use *refute* in your news writing only if there is a consensus that the denial has been successful. Don't make the judgment on your own.

reluctant/reticent   Don't be sheepish about enforcing this distinction. People who are reluctant to do something are not necessarily reticent. A *reluctant* person is unwilling to do something:

> For reasons she would not disclose, Thomason was <u>reluctant</u> to declare her candidacy for the city council.

If a person is unwilling to speak readily or is uncommonly reserved, we generally describe that individual as *reticent*:

The professor has instituted a class for <u>reticent</u> speakers.

renown/renowned   Often confused, these two words are different parts of speech. *Renown*, a noun, means "fame or eminence"; *renowned*, an adjective, means "famous or celebrated":

She is a motivational speaker of great <u>renown</u>.
(noun—obj. of prep.)

Nobel laureate Linus Pauling was <u>renowned</u> for his groundbreaking
(pred. adj.)
work in chemistry.

restrictive/nonrestrictive   A *restrictive clause* is an essential clause that helps control the meaning of a sentence. Understanding this helps you in at least two ways:

1. The restrictive clause does not need to be set off by commas.

2. In a choice between *that* and *which, that* is always the correct pronoun subject or object for the restrictive clause.

    A campfire <u>that got out of control in the Gifford Pinchot National Forest two days ago</u> is now threatening two nearby towns.

A *nonrestrictive clause*, however, is not essential to the full meaning of a sentence. This clause *must* be set off by commas, and you use *which* instead of *that* when the choice has to be made:

The Gifford Pinchot fire, <u>which thus far has consumed 800 acres of old-growth timber</u>, may be brought under control by this weekend, according to USDA Forest Service officials.

See also entry for *that/which/who.*

run-on sentence   Like the tedious infomercial, it doesn't know when to stop. The run-on may actually be a jumble of sentences because of improper punctuation:

Picket lines went up for a fourth straight day, nurses vowed to continue to honor them until contract talks resume.

Use a semicolon instead of a comma or insert the conjunction *and* after the comma to correct this fault. See also the entry for *comma splice* and p. 53.

said   Don't overlook the obvious when quoting someone in your writing. Searching for variety in reporting how someone said something, writers

RE-SA

sometimes grasp at *stated, uttered, elucidated, declared* or what have you. Describing the speaker and his or her delivery is more important than poring over a thesaurus to find a verb that is better off in a game of Scrabble than in your writing.

semicolon   This punctuation mark helps you avoid the run-on sentence. When two independent clauses are in one sentence and are not separated by a conjunction such as *or, but* or *and,* they must be separated by a semicolon:

> This is not your ordinary, barn-twirling tornado; it is the perfect storm.

When two independent clauses are joined by a conjunctive adverb such as *however, nevertheless* or *therefore,* a semicolon also is needed:

> I cannot support this committee's recommendation; however, I plan to abstain rather than cast a negative vote.

SE-SI

sentence   A *sentence* is one or more independent clauses that present a complete thought. Sorry to say, writers do awful things to sentences: They make one run into another, they clutter them with unnecessary punctuation and sometimes they neglect to put a verb in one but still call it a sentence:

> Such as this fragment.

A good sentence is an enlightenment, a forceful directive, an amusing bit of play. But it is always well-contained; its thought is always complete. See Chapter 5.

set/sit   Normally the verb *set* requires an object:

> Please set the package on the table.

Sit, however, *never* takes an object:

> Would you like to sit down?

since/because   These words are not synonymous. *Since* is properly used when it denotes a period of time, whether continuous or broken:

> How long has it been since you've had an old-fashioned lemon phosphate?

Because gives a reason or cause:

> I refuse to sign this petition because it would limit our First Amendment freedoms.

Note that in most circumstances a comma is not needed before *because.*

split constructions   The split infinitive is always a handy target for grammarians. However, the chief reason for objecting to the split infinitive—loss of clarity—is also the reason for avoiding unnecessary splits of a subject and a verb and of a verb and its complement. Some examples:

> The Secretary of Defense has agreed <u>to</u> before the start of the next Congressional session <u>reveal</u> the nature of troop buildups in the Gulf region.
> (Insertion of two prepositional phrases between the two parts of the infinitive is both awkward and sloppy.)

> <u>Smithfield</u>, before switching to the Praktika line of single-lens reflex photo equipment and commercially endorsing it at great profit to himself, <u>used</u> "plate cameras" early in his career.
> (A split between subject and verb—although not unusual—can be awkward when a lengthy split causes the reader to lose track of the thought.)

> The prime minister has reportedly <u>rejected</u>, in a secret meeting with European Union diplomats held just yesterday morning, <u>the most recent European trade agreement</u> with several Balkan states.
> (A split between the verb and its complement disturbs the natural flow by injecting lengthy explanatory material.)

SP-TH

than/then   *Then*—an adverb denoting time—is often confused with than. If you are comparing something, use *than:*

> No one is more aware of America's breakfast habits <u>than</u> our fast-food franchise executives.

Then, on the other hand, carries the sense of "soon afterward":

> Let's visit our favorite café and have caramel lattes; <u>then</u> we can head to the gym to suffer at the hands of our aerobics instructor.
> (Note that *then* cannot connect these two independent clauses on its own. A semicolon is needed.)

When *than* is used to introduce an implied clause of comparison, the pronoun that may follow is most likely in the nominative case:

> Tom is a lot smarter <u>than I</u> [am smart].

But some sentences won't permit this implied arrangement:

> There is not a more dedicated volunteer <u>than her.</u>
> ("Than she is a volunteer" would not make sense here.)

that/which/who   As the entry for *restrictive/nonrestrictive* says, *that* is used to restrict meaning and *which* is used to elaborate on it. These pronouns are used only in their particular types of clauses, but *who* can be used in both types when it refers to people or to things endowed by the writer with human qualities:

My recipes that require soy products are all filed next to the microwave oven.
(restrictive—comma not needed)

Construction bonds, which can be a dependable tax shelter, carry different interest rates according to the credit standing of the local government.
(nonrestrictive—gives explanation, and a comma is required)

The demonstrators who interrupted the senator's speech were arrested.
(restrictive—in this case, *who* is preferred over *that* because we are talking about real people, not inanimate objects or concepts. Again, a comma is not required.)

Newland, who is running for the state Senate seat from Medford, charged this morning that the governor's office has been "grossly mismanaged."
(nonrestrictive—explanatory material follows *who.* Note the inclusion of commas.)

See also pgs. 101–102 and the entry for *restrictive/nonrestrictive.*

their/there/they're Although they sound alike, they are (they're!) quite different. *Their* is the possessive form of the pronoun *they:*

Their presentation is scheduled for 3 p.m.
(*Their* modifies the noun *presentation.*)

When it begins a sentence, *there* is called an *expletive.* It is sometimes called a *false subject* because it doesn't help determine the number of the verb:

There are many reasons to deny your petition.
(Note that the noun *reasons,* not *there,* controls the number of the verb.)

They're is a contraction of *they* and *are,* used only informally when you want to combine subject and verb:

"They're ready for you, Mr. President," the aide announced.

there are/there is Beginning a sentence with the expletive *there* is generally an indirect and ineffective way to communicate. It adds clutter rather than meaning. When you have to use it, however, be aware that *there* is not the subject of the sentence and does not control the number of the verb. In these sentences the subject usually follows the verb and controls its number:

There are many ways to fend off bankruptcy.

Generally speaking, only the first part of a compound subject following the verb in these sentences is used to determine the number of the verb:

There is too much waste and inefficiency in this company.
(verb)   (subj.)   (subj.)

toward/towards   Dictionaries call *towards* "archaic and rare." Save it for an antique convention.

try and/try to   Writing is more precise than speech. Although we may say—and hear—such a sentence as "She will try and pass the test," this is not proper language use. When we write that someone is *attempting* something, we do not mean that the person is both trying *and* doing; we mean the person is trying *to* do something. It makes sense to introduce the infinitive with the preposition *to:*

He told the reporters that he would try to reach the stranded climbers by nightfall.

TO-VE

unique   Why is this adjective regularly adorned with superficial and redundant words, as in "most unique" or "very unique"? *Unique* means, simply, "the only one of its kind." Don't succumb to word inflation or to the embarrassing overstatement that it reveals.

up   It can be anything but upbeat when it is coupled with a verb. Phrases such as *face up, slow up* and *head up* are clutter:

He must face up to the growing conflict in his department.

Why can't this person just face the conflict?

verb and verbals   The *verb* is the very life of a sentence. It breathes, sings, squeezes, inspires; it drives all the other sentence parts. When chosen correctly, it is in command. Pick your verbs wisely; they can take you far. *Verbals*, however are *not verbs* (can we be any more direct than that?). They are participial phrases, infinitives and gerunds. Although verbals sometimes have the *feel* of action, that is mainly related to the *-ing* endings on many of them and to the apparent verb form that follows *to* in infinitives. Don't be fooled: Verbals do not control the movement of a sentence. See p. 25.

very   Be very wary of *very* when you are tempted to give an adjective more punch. If you get used to the practice, you might overlook better, more precise adjectives and contribute to clutter. *Very* is but one example of an overused intensifier. Others are *really, completely, extremely* and *totally.* For example, rather than describe someone as *very sad,* you could choose among these words: *depressed, melancholy, sorrowful* or *doleful.* See p. 150.

who's/whose   If you want the subject–verb contraction, use *who's:*

Who's buying the tofu burritos tonight?
(Who is buying ...)

If you need the possessive pronoun, use *whose:*

Whose turn is it to buy the tofu burritos tonight?

If you want to use *whose,* it must modify something directly or by implication. In the preceding sentence, *whose* modifies the noun *turn.*

who/whom   Although informal, "shopping mall" speech has done its best to eliminate *whom* from this handsome pair of pronouns, the case for their "distinction with a difference" remains strong. In most writing situations, the use of *whom* does not seem elitist; it is merely correct:

Whom did the mayor name to her campaign committee?

The use of *whom* (the objective case of *who*) shows the reader that the pronoun receives the action of the verb rather than initiates it.

The jockey who the Thoroughbred Association said had thrown the race was cleared today by the state Racing Commission.

A breakdown of this sentence reveals that *who had thrown the race* is a subordinate clause and that *the Association said* is for attribution only. Obviously, proper selection of *who* and *whom* shows that you are a writer who understands the function of sentence parts. If you also want to utter such sentences as "Whom did you wish to see?" when someone comes to your door, well, that's up to you.

your/you're   The distinctions made in the entries for *their/there/they're* and *who's/whose* apply here. If you want to use the possessive form of the personal pronoun *you,* use *your:*

Your Freudian slips are showing.
(*Your* modifies the noun *slips.*)

If you want to compress (contract) the subject-verb *you are,* use *you're:*

You're going to be a great writer!

INDEX